Holiday
family favorites

Pork Chops, Cabbage
& Apples, page 99

Holiday
family favorites

Oxmoor
House®

Holiday
family favorites

©2010 by Gooseberry Patch
2500 Farmers Drive, Suite 110, Columbus, OH 43235
1-800-854-6673, **www.gooseberrypatch.com**
©2010 by Time Home Entertainment Inc.
135 West 50th Street, New York, NY 10020

ISBN-13: 978-0-8487-3414-5
ISBN-10: 0-8487-3414-9
Library of Congress Control Number: 2009941688
Printed in the United States of America
First Printing 2010

Oxmoor House
VP, Publishing Director: Jim Childs
Editorial Director: Susan Payne Dobbs
Brand Manager: Terri Laschober Robertson
Senior Editor: Rebecca Brennan
Managing Editor: Laurie S. Herr

Gooseberry Patch Homestyle Family Favorites
Editor: Georgia Dodge
Project Editor: Emily Chappell
Senior Designer: Melissa Jones Clark
Director, Test Kitchens: Elizabeth Tyler Austin
Assistant Director, Test Kitchens: Julie Christopher
Test Kitchens Professionals: Allison E. Cox, Julie Gunter,
    Kathleen Royal Phillips, Catherine Crowell Steele,
    Ashley T. Strickland
Photography Director: Jim Bathie
Senior Photo Stylist: Kay E. Clarke
Associate Photo Stylist: Katherine Eckert Coyne
Senior Production Manager: Greg A. Amason

Contributors
Designer: Nancy Johnson
Copy Editor: Jasmine Hodges
Proofreader: Norma Buttersworth McKittrick
Interns: Sarah Bélanger, Allison Sperando,
    Caitlin Watzke

Time Home Entertainment Inc.
Publisher: Richard Fraiman
General Manager: Steven Sandonato
Executive Director, Marketing Services: Carol Pittard
Executive Director, Retail and Special Sales: Tom Mifsud
Director, New Product Development: Peter Harper
Director, Publicity: Sydney Webber
Assistant Director, Newsstand Marketing: Laura Adam
Assistant Publishing Director, Brand Marketing: Joy Butts
Associate Counsel: Helen Wan

To order additional publications, call 1-800-765-6400 or 1-800-491-0551.

For more books to enrich your life, visit **oxmoorhouse.com**
To search, savor, and share thousands of recipes, visit **myrecipes.com**

Cover: Festive Pork Roasts (page 101), Au Gratin Potato Casserole (page 164), Cranberry Relish Salad (page 173)
Page 1: Cranberry-Pecan Coffee Cakes (page 287)

Dear Friend,

What's the best way to enjoy the holidays? With family, friends & food, of course! Whether it's a big Thanksgiving feast or a picnic on the 4th of July, there's always an occasion to get together with loved ones, and we've got all the recipes you need to make your celebrations special throughout the year!

Invite friends over for a casual New Year's Day dinner of Hearty Black-Eyed Peas (page 61) and cooked cabbage. This tasty twosome is thought to bring good luck and prosperity in the coming year. On Easter Sunday, try Mark's Egg Salad Sandwiches (page 135) instead of the traditional baked ham…they're simply delightful. Don't forget to celebrate Mom & Dad in the summer months! Spinach-Cheddar Quiche (page 104) is perfect for a Mothers' Day brunch, and Grilled Cuban Sandwiches (page 143) are just right for a Fathers' Day lunch. Gather 'round the breakfast table on Christmas morning for delicious Cheese & Chile Casserole (page 76) and Streusel Cran-Orange Muffins (page 207)…the savory and sweet combination is so good, you'll be asking for thirds! From appetizers, soups and sides to main dishes, desserts and edible gifts, we've included all of the best recipes for these holidays and more!

Take a look inside…you'll also find lots of how-to's and clever ideas for all of your gatherings. And to help you prepare for your celebration meals, we've tagged each recipe with a holiday banner, though we're sure you'll enjoy them all year-round! No matter the celebration, *Holiday Family Favorites* is sure to inspire your holiday plans.

Wishing you warm memories & good food!

Vickie & JoAnn

Contents

30-Minute Chili, page 131

Apple-Broccoli Salad, page 183

9 Festive Party Starters
*tasty appetizers, kid-friendly snacks
& refreshing beverages*

39 Casual Get-Togethers
*no-fuss dishes to serve throughout
the year*

75 Memorable Main Dishes
*special-occasion recipes for your
favorite celebrations*

115 Savory Soups &
Sandwiches
easy & delicious ideas for entertaining

147 Splendid Sides & Salads
*superb selections for rounding out
every meal*

187 Bountiful Breads
sweet & savory breads for every occasion

Scalloped Potatoes with Ham, page 163

Bread Pudding, page 249

217 Divine Desserts
sweet endings to any meal

267 Giftable Goodies
homemade gifts from the kitchen

307 Celebration Menus
16 seasonal menus for every holiday

317 Index
find any recipe...fast

320 Our Story
how Gooseberry Patch got started

Baked Spinach & Artichoke Dip, page 26

festive party starters

A holiday get-together wouldn't be complete without a few tasty beverages, appetizers and kid-approved snacks! Gather 'round the fire on a chilly December night and warm up with a cup of Snow Cocoa (page 10). Heading to a New Year's Eve party? Bring along Baked Spinach & Artichoke Dip (page 26). No matter what time of year you serve them, these festive party starters will be a hit! Look for the holiday banner above each recipe to guide you in planning your next celebration.

Pineapple Wassail

Bring to a holiday open house while warm…mmmm.

4 c. unsweetened pineapple juice

12-oz. can apricot nectar

2 c. apple cider

1½ c. orange juice

2 (3-inch) cinnamon sticks

1 t. whole cloves

4 cardamom seeds, crushed

Combine ingredients in a 3-quart saucepan; heat to boiling. Reduce heat and simmer 15 to 20 minutes; strain into serving glasses or punch bowl. Serve warm. Makes about 2 quarts.

Snow Cocoa

Stir together this cocoa in the slow cooker and plug in before heading out to go sledding!

2 c. whipping cream

6 c. milk

1 t. vanilla extract

12-oz. pkg. white chocolate chips

Combine all ingredients in a 3-quart slow cooker. Cover and cook on low setting 2 to 2½ hours or until chocolate is melted and mixture is hot. Stir well to blend. Serves 10.

Kendall Hale
Lynn, MA

Sweet Almond Coffee

Enjoy this sweet cocoa-almond blend on a frosty night.

½ c. sugar
¼ c. baking cocoa
¼ c. instant coffee granules
¼ c. finely ground almonds

2 t. powdered non-dairy creamer
¼ t. salt
4½ c. milk

In an electric blender, combine sugar, cocoa, instant coffee, almonds, creamer and salt. Cover and blend on high speed 10 seconds. Heat milk in a 2-quart saucepan. Do not boil. Add cocoa mixture to hot milk; stir to combine. Pour into mugs. Makes 5 cups.

Vickie
Gooseberry Patch

make it special

Set out whipped cream and shakers of cinnamon and cocoa at dessert time for coffee drinkers. Tea drinkers will love a basket of special teas with honey and lemon slices. Special desserts deserve the best!

Peppermint Milkshakes

This yummy dessert drink appeals to all ages. Use less milk for really thick shakes.

8 c. vanilla ice cream, divided

2 c. milk, divided

1 c. crushed hard peppermint round candies (about 40 to 50 candies), divided

8½-oz. can refrigerated instant whipped cream

Garnish: peppermint sticks

Process 4 cups ice cream, one cup milk and ½ cup crushed candies in a blender until smooth, stopping to scrape down sides as needed. Pour into small serving glasses; top with whipped cream and place a peppermint stick in each glass. Repeat with remaining ingredients. Makes 9¼ cups.

Note: Process peppermint candies in a food processor for quick crushing.

Homemade Eggnog

Sprinkle with cinnamon or nutmeg before serving.

There's nothing
like the taste
of homemade
eggnog!
Rebecca

⅔ c. sugar
4 egg yolks
½ t. salt
4 c. milk
8 c. half-and-half
nutmeg to taste

1 pt. whipping cream, chilled
3 T. sugar
2 t. vanilla extract
Optional: frozen whipped
    topping, thawed, and
    cinnamon or nutmeg

Beat sugar into egg yolks in a saucepan; add salt and stir in milk. Cook mixture over medium heat, stirring constantly, until mixture coats the back of a metal spoon. Remove from heat and set pan in ice water to cool quickly. Pour through a sieve to remove lumps. Add half-and-half to cooled mixture; sprinkle with nutmeg. In a separate bowl, whip cream with sugar and vanilla; fold into egg mixture. Stir well before serving. Garnish with a dollop of whipped topping and a sprinkle of cinnamon or nutmeg, if desired. Serves 12.

Rebecca Ferguson
Carlisle, AR

4th of July

Iced Mint Tea

4 c. water
1 c. sugar
⅓ c. lemon juice
2 family-size tea bags

1 c. fresh mint leaves, loosely
    packed
4 c. cold water
ice cubes

Bring 4 cups water to a boil in a saucepan over medium-high heat. Stir in sugar and cook, stirring constantly, one minute or until sugar dissolves; remove from heat. Stir in lemon juice, tea bags and mint leaves. Cover and let stand 10 minutes. Remove tea bags. Cover and let stand 40 minutes.

Pour tea mixture through a wire-mesh strainer into a 2-quart pitcher, discarding mint leaves. Stir in cold water. Cover and chill at least one hour. Serve over ice. Makes 8½ cups.

New Year's

Citrus Mimosa

1 c. prepared strawberry
    daiquiri mix
¾ c. cold water
6-oz. can frozen orange juice
    concentrate, thawed
¾ c. fresh grapefruit juice

⅓ c. frozen lemonade
    concentrate, thawed
3 T. frozen limeade concentrate,
    thawed
1 bottle champagne, chilled
Optional: orange zest curls

Makes the champagne go a little further! If you prefer, substitute carbonated water for the champagne.
Vickie

Combine prepared daiquiri mix, water, orange juice concentrate, grapefruit juice, lemonade and limeade concentrates in a pitcher or bowl. Stir until well combined. Cover and chill. To serve, pour an equal amount of the chilled mixture and champagne into each glass. Garnish with orange zest curls, if desired. Serves 8.

Vickie
Gooseberry Patch

Caramelized Vidalia Onion Dip

Here's a new take on an old favorite appetizer. Look for sturdy sweet potato chips for scooping up this mega-cheesy family favorite.

2 T. butter
3 Vidalia or other sweet onions,
    thinly sliced
8-oz. pkg. cream cheese,
    softened

8-oz. pkg. Swiss cheese,
    shredded
1 c. grated Parmesan cheese
1 c. mayonnaise
sweet potato chips

Melt butter in a large skillet over medium heat; add sliced onions. Cook, stirring often, 30 to 40 minutes or until onions are caramel colored.

Combine onions, cheeses and mayonnaise, stirring well. Spoon dip into a lightly greased 1½- to 2-quart casserole dish. Bake, uncovered, at 375 degrees for 30 minutes or until golden and bubbly. Serve with sweet potato chips. Makes 4 cups.

homemade tortilla chips

Make your own tortilla chips to go with salsas and dips...you won't believe how easy it is. Just slice flour tortillas into wedges, spray with non-stick vegetable spray and bake at 350 degrees for 5 to 7 minutes.

Aloha Chicken Wings

A staple at any gathering.

¼ c. butter
½ c. catsup
1 clove garlic, minced
3 lbs. chicken wings
1 c. bread crumbs
14-oz. can pineapple chunks,
    drained and juice reserved

2 T. brown sugar, packed
1 T. fresh ginger, minced
1 T. Worcestershire sauce
hot pepper sauce to taste

Place butter in a 15"x10" jelly-roll pan; heat in a 400-degree oven until melted. Stir together catsup and garlic; brush over wings. Coat with bread crumbs; arrange in pan, turning to coat both sides with melted butter. Bake at 400 degrees for 30 minutes. While baking, add enough water to reserved pineapple juice to equal ¾ cup liquid; pour into a small mixing bowl. Whisk in remaining ingredients; pour over wings. Continue baking until juices run clear when chicken is pierced with a fork, about 20 to 30 more minutes. Place pineapple chunks around wings, baking until heated through. Serves 4.

Dianne Gregory
Sheridan, AR

stack it up

Use tiered cake stands for bite-size appetizers…so handy, and they take up less space on the buffet table than setting out several serving platters.

Curly Pigtails

10 (12-inch) wooden skewers
10 all-beef hot dogs
½ c. mustard
2 t. brown sugar, packed

1 t. curry powder
8-oz. can refrigerated crescent
rolls

Insert a wooden skewer into one end of each hot dog, leaving 7 inches of each skewer exposed. Combine mustard, sugar and curry powder in a small bowl, stirring well.

Unroll crescent roll dough and shape into a 12"x8" rectangle. Press perforations to seal. Cut rectangle evenly into 10 (8-inch-long) strips.

Brush one side of each strip with mustard mixture. Wrap one strip around each hot dog, mustard side in, leaving ¾ inch of the hot dog exposed as dough forms a spiral. Place on an ungreased baking sheet. Bake at 375 degrees for 10 to 12 minutes or until golden. Serve with remaining mustard mixture. Serves 10.

Ultimate Nachos

⅓ c. onion, finely chopped
1 clove garlic, minced
1 T. olive oil
16-oz. can refried beans
½ c. salsa
13-oz. pkg. restaurant-style
   tortilla chips
1½ c. shredded Monterey Jack
   cheese
1½ c. shredded Cheddar cheese
pickled jalapeño slices, well
   drained
Optional: 1 c. guacamole,
   ½ c. sour cream
Optional: chopped fresh cilantro,
   sliced ripe olives, shredded
   lettuce, additional salsa

Sauté onion and garlic in hot oil in a skillet over medium heat 4 to 5 minutes or until onion is tender. Add beans and salsa to pan, stirring until beans are creamy. Cook one minute or until heated.

Scatter most of chips on a parchment paper-lined large baking sheet or an oven-proof platter. Top with bean mixture, cheeses and desired amount of jalapeños.

Bake at 450 degrees for 8 minutes or until cheeses melt and edges are golden.

Top with small dollops of guacamole and sour cream, if desired. Add desired toppings. Serve hot. Serves 6 to 8.

tailgating fun

Everybody loves a tailgating party…and a small-town college rivalry can be just as much fun as a Big Ten game. Load up a pickup truck with tasty finger foods, sandwich fixin's and a big washtub full of bottled drinks on ice. It's all about food and fun!

Ham-Cream Cheese Croissants

1½ c. cooked ham, cubed
8-oz. pkg. cream cheese,
    softened

8-oz. tube refrigerated
    crescent rolls

In a medium mixing bowl, combine ham and cream cheese.
Unroll and separate crescent rolls; place a dollop of ham mixture
on each croissant. Roll up and place on an ungreased baking sheet.
Bake, uncovered, at 425 degrees for 15 to 18 minutes. Serves 8.

Donna Vogel
The Colony, TX

Brie Kisses

⅔ lb. Brie cheese
17.3-oz. pkg. frozen puff pastry

red hot pepper jelly

Cut Brie into 32 (½-inch) cubes; arrange on a plate and place in the
freezer. Let pastry thaw at room temperature 30 minutes; unfold each
pastry and roll with a rolling pin to remove creases. Slice each sheet
into quarters; slice each quarter in half. Cut each piece in half one
more time for a total of 32 squares. Place squares into greased mini
muffin cups; arrange so corners of dough point upward. Bake at
400 degrees for 5 minutes. Place one Brie cube in center of each
pastry. Bake 10 minutes or until edges are golden. Remove from pan.
Immediately top with pepper jelly. Makes 32.

Kathy Grashoff
Fort Wayne, IN

Roasted Red Pepper Bruschetta

Top these toasts with a sweet-tangy roasted red pepper mix and feta cheese. The combination makes a pretty hors d'oeuvre for a holiday party.

12-oz. jar roasted red peppers, drained and finely chopped
½ c. plum tomato, finely chopped
¼ c. red onion, finely chopped
2 T. balsamic vinegar
6 T. olive oil, divided

½ t. salt
½ t. pepper
⅛ t. sugar
1 baguette, cut into 28 slices
salt and pepper to taste
½ c. crumbled garlic and herb-flavored feta cheese

Combine first 3 ingredients in a bowl. Combine vinegar, 2 tablespoons olive oil, salt, pepper and sugar; pour over roasted pepper mixture and toss well. Cover and chill up to a day.

When ready to serve, arrange baguette slices on a large ungreased baking sheet. Brush or drizzle slices with ¼ cup olive oil. Sprinkle with salt and pepper. Bake at 400 degrees for 4 minutes or until lightly toasted. Spoon about one tablespoon pepper mixture onto each baguette slice; top each with cheese. Broil 5½ inches from heat 3 minutes or until bubbly and lightly golden. Serve warm. Makes 28.

for parties...

Fill different baskets with dippers and snacks like pretzels, bagel chips, veggies, bread cubes and potato chips. Use a small riser (a book works well) to set under one side of the bottom of each basket to create a tilt...looks so nice, and guests can grab the food easily!

Spicy Crawfish Spread

*Serve this sassy Cajun spread with corn chips, vegetable crudités
or crackers.*

3 T. butter
¾ c. onion, finely diced
¾ c. celery, finely diced
4 cloves garlic, minced
2 T. salt-free seasoning
½ t. cayenne pepper

8 oz. peeled, cooked crawfish
   tails, chopped
8-oz. pkg. cream cheese,
   softened
Optional: celery leaf

Melt butter in a small skillet over medium-high heat. Add onion,
celery and garlic; sauté 5 minutes or until onion and celery are tender.
Add seasoning and pepper; sauté 30 seconds. Combine sautéed
vegetables and crawfish tails in a bowl. Add softened cream cheese
and stir gently to combine. Garnish with a celery leaf, if desired.
Makes 2¼ cups.

dippers

Try serving "light" dippers with hearty full-flavored dips and
spreads. Fresh veggies, pita wedges, baked tortilla strips
and multi-grain crispbread are all sturdy enough to scoop up
dips yet won't overshadow the flavor of the dip.

Baked Spinach & Artichoke Dip

(pictured on page 8)

2 (6-oz.) pkgs. fresh baby
   spinach
1 T. butter
8-oz. pkg. Neufchâtel cheese
1 clove garlic, chopped

14-oz. can artichoke hearts,
   drained and chopped
½ c. light sour cream
½ c. shredded part-skim
   mozzarella cheese, divided

Microwave spinach in a large microwave-safe bowl on high
3 minutes or until wilted; drain well. Press spinach between paper
towels to remove excess moisture. Chop spinach.

Melt butter in a non-stick skillet over medium-high heat. Add
Neufchâtel cheese and garlic; cook 3 to 4 minutes, stirring constantly,
until cream cheese melts. Fold in spinach, artichokes, sour cream and
¼ cup mozzarella cheese; stir until mozzarella cheese melts.

Transfer mixture to a shallow one-quart casserole dish. Sprinkle
with remaining ¼ cup mozzarella cheese. Bake at 350 degrees for
15 minutes or until hot and bubbly. Serve immediately with fresh
pita wedges or baked pita chips. Serves 11.

make it ahead!

For easy entertaining, assemble this dish a day ahead. Cover and store in the
refrigerator. Uncover and bake just before serving.

Yuletide Crab Puffs

These savory puffs can be made ahead of time and frozen or stored in an airtight container until ready to fill. The filling can be made several hours in advance and spooned into the puffs just before serving.

1 lb. fresh lump crabmeat,
    drained and flaked
1½ c. mayonnaise
⅔ c. celery, chopped
½ c. onion, chopped
4 eggs, hard-boiled, peeled and
    chopped
1 T. fresh parsley, minced

2 T. chili sauce
½ t. salt
½ t. pepper
1 c. boiling water
½ c. butter or margarine, cut
    into pieces
1 c. all-purpose flour
4 eggs, lightly beaten

Combine first 9 ingredients. Cover and chill filling.

Combine boiling water and butter in a medium bowl; stir until butter melts. Add flour and stir vigorously until mixture leaves sides of bowl and forms a smooth ball. Let mixture cool 2 minutes. Add eggs, beating vigorously with a wooden spoon until dough is smooth. Drop by teaspoonfuls onto an ungreased baking sheet.

Bake at 400 degrees for 25 minutes or until puffed and golden; remove puffs from pan and cool on a wire rack. Cut top off each puff, using a serrated knife. Fill each puff with a heaping tablespoon of filling and replace top. Makes 2 dozen.

Note: Puffs may appear done before baking time is completed, but they may fall if they're taken out of the oven too soon.

Stuffed Strawberries

Stuffed Strawberries

Try using pecans in place of the walnuts for added variety.

20 strawberries, hulled and
    divided
8-oz. pkg. cream cheese,
    softened

¼ c. walnuts, finely chopped
1 T. powdered sugar
Optional: fresh mint leaves

    Dice 2 strawberries; set aside. Cut a thin layer from the stem end of the remaining strawberries, forming a base. Starting at opposite end of strawberry, slice into 4 wedges, being careful not to slice through the base; set aside.

    Beat remaining ingredients together until fluffy; fold in diced strawberries. Spoon 1½ tablespoonfuls into the center of each strawberry. Refrigerate until ready to serve. Garnish with fresh mint leaves, if desired. Makes 18.

Barbara Parham Hyde
Manchester, TN

Pineapple Ball

2 (8-oz.) pkgs. cream cheese,
    softened
2 T. green pepper, chopped
2 T. onion, finely chopped

2 t. seasoned salt
¼ c. crushed pineapple, drained
2 T. sugar
2 c. chopped pecans, divided

    Mix first 6 ingredients with one cup pecans; shape into a ball. Cover and chill one hour. Roll in remaining pecans; cover with plastic wrap and refrigerate until firm. Makes about 2½ cups.

Janice Patterson
Black Forest, CO

Serve this with an assortment of crackers and bread sticks and watch it disappear!

Janice

Mothers' Day

Egg Salad Crostini

3 T. cream cheese, softened
2 to 3 T. mayonnaise
2 t. honey mustard
¼ t. hot pepper sauce
3 eggs, hard-boiled and chopped

½ c. green olives with pimentos,
　coarsely chopped
⅓ c. celery, finely chopped
1 T. onion, minced
Optional: fresh parsley sprigs

Beat cream cheese, mayonnaise, honey mustard and hot pepper sauce at low speed with an electric mixer just until smooth.

Add eggs, olives, celery and onion; toss gently. Cover and chill mixture thoroughly. (Egg salad mixture can be made a day ahead and kept in refrigerator.) To serve, spoon one tablespoon egg salad onto each crostino. Garnish with fresh parsley sprigs, if desired. Makes one dozen.

Crostino:

¼ French baguette

3 T. butter or margarine, melted

Slice baguette into 12 thin slices (about ¼-inch thick). Brush top of each slice generously with melted butter. Place on an ungreased baking sheet. Bake at 400 degrees for 10 minutes or until crisp and golden. Let cool. May be stored in an airtight container up to one week. Makes one dozen.

New Year's

Black-Eyed Caviar

2 (15-oz.) cans black-eyed peas, drained
1 yellow or green pepper, finely chopped
½ c. roasted red peppers packed in oil, drained and finely chopped
½ c. red onion, minced
½ c. fresh cilantro or parsley, minced

¼ c. olive oil
2 cloves garlic, minced
2 T. white wine vinegar
1 t. ground cumin
2 t. coarse-grain mustard
¼ t. salt
pita chips

Combine all ingredients in a medium-size bowl; stir well. Cover and chill several hours. Serve at room temperature with pita chips. Makes 4½ cups.

4th of July

Chunky Guacamole

3 ripe avocados, coarsely chopped
½ c. sour cream
2 T. mayonnaise
⅓ c. tomato, finely chopped
4-oz. can chopped green chiles, drained

4 green onions, chopped
2 T. lime juice
2 t. chili powder
¾ t. salt

Combine avocado, sour cream and mayonnaise in a large bowl. Mash just until blended.

Add tomato and remaining ingredients; stir just until blended. Cover and chill. Makes 4 cups.

Fresh Salsa

Fresh Salsa

1 jalapeño pepper, seeded and
    minced
1 cucumber, peeled and diced
4 plum tomatoes, chopped
½ c. fresh cilantro, finely
    chopped

2 T. vinegar
2 T. olive oil
1 t. sugar
1 t. ground cumin
½ t. salt
tortilla chips

Stir together all ingredients except tortilla chips in a small
bowl. Cover and chill at least one hour. Serve with tortilla chips.
Makes 3½ cups.

Curried Chicken Salad Tea Sandwiches

4 c. cooked chicken, finely
    chopped
3 (8-oz.) pkgs. cream cheese,
    softened
¾ c. dried cranberries, chopped
½ c. sweetened flaked coconut,
    toasted
6 green onions, minced

2 stalks celery, diced
2¼-oz. pkg. slivered almonds,
    toasted
1 T. curry powder
1 T. fresh ginger, grated
½ t. salt
½ t. pepper
48 slices whole-grain bread

Stir together all ingredients except bread. Spread mixture on one
side each of 24 bread slices; top with remaining 24 bread slices. Trim
crusts from sandwiches; cut each sandwich into 4 rectangles with a
serrated knife. Makes about 2 dozen.

Black Bean Tartlets

1¼ c. all-purpose flour
¾ c. yellow cornmeal
½ c. shredded Monterey Jack
    cheese with peppers
1 t. salt
1 t. ground cumin
1 t. chili powder
½ t. garlic powder

½ t. cayenne pepper
½ c. cold butter or margarine,
    cut into pieces
1 egg, lightly beaten
2 T. ice water
Optional: sour cream, fresh
    cilantro

Process first 8 ingredients in a food processor until blended. Add butter and process until mixture is crumbly. Add egg and ice water; process just until mixture forms a ball.

Divide dough in half; shape each half of dough into 16 (1-inch) balls. Press balls into lightly greased mini muffin cups, pressing evenly into bottom and up sides.

Bake tartlet shells at 450 degrees for 8 minutes or until lightly browned. Cool in pans 10 minutes; remove shells to wire racks and cool completely.

When ready to serve, spoon one tablespoon Black Bean Salsa into each tartlet shell; garnish with sour cream and fresh cilantro, if desired. Serve at room temperature. Makes 32 appetizers.

Black Bean Salsa:

15-oz. can black beans, drained
2 canned chipotle chiles in
    adobo sauce, minced
3 green onions, chopped
½ c. yellow pepper, finely
    chopped

1 plum tomato, finely chopped
1 T. fresh cilantro, chopped
2 T. lime juice
1 T. olive oil
½ t. salt

Combine all ingredients in a bowl, tossing well. Cover and chill at least one hour. Makes 2¼ cups.

Jo Ann
Gooseberry Patch

Not-Your-Usual Party Mix

15.6-oz. pkg. crispy rice cereal
   squares
10-oz. pkg. oyster crackers
9½-oz. pkg. mini cheese-filled
   sandwich crackers
6-oz. pkg. fish-shaped crackers

16-oz. pkg. mini pretzel twists
16-oz. pkg. peanuts
12-oz. bottle butter-flavored
   popcorn oil
1-oz. pkg. ranch salad
   dressing mix

*A tasty munchie
no one can resist!*
Samantha

Combine cereal, crackers, pretzels and peanuts in a large bowl.
Combine oil and salad dressing mix in a small bowl; toss with
cracker mixture until evenly coated. Store in an airtight container.
Serves 20.

Samantha Starks
Madison, WI

Puppy Chow Snack Mix…For People!

For a tasty variation, use butterscotch chips in place of chocolate chips.

8 oz. bite-size crispy rice cereal
   squares
½ c. butter

6-oz. pkg. chocolate chips
½ c. peanut butter
2 c. powdered sugar

Place cereal squares in a large bowl. Melt butter, chocolate chips
and peanut butter together. Pour over cereal squares and mix well. Pour
sugar into a paper bag; pour cereal mixture into bag and shake. Store
finished snack in a plastic zipping bag. Makes about 8 cups.

Barb Agne
Delaware, OH

Caramel Apples

Caramel apples are the stuff of fall festivals and Halloween carnivals!
With each messy bite, they bring out the child in us all.

6 Granny Smith apples
6 wooden craft sticks
14-oz. pkg. caramels,
   unwrapped
1 T. vanilla extract
1 T. water

2 c. chopped pecans or peanuts,
   toasted
Optional: 12-oz. bag semi-sweet
   chocolate chips, pecan
   halves

Wash and dry apples; remove stems. Insert a craft stick into stem end of each apple; set aside.

Combine caramels, vanilla and water in a microwave-safe bowl. Microwave on high 90 seconds or until melted, stirring twice.

Dip each apple into the caramel mixture quickly, allowing excess caramel to drip off. Roll in chopped nuts; place apples on lightly greased wax paper. Chill at least 15 minutes.

If desired, to make chocolate-dipped caramel apples, microwave chocolate chips on high 90 seconds or until melted, stirring twice; cool 5 minutes. Pour chocolate where craft sticks and apples meet, allowing chocolate to drip down sides of caramel apples. Press pecan halves onto chocolate, if desired. Chill 15 minutes or until set. Makes 6 apples.

fall treats

After wrapping each apple in cellophane, nestle it inside a small orange gift sack. Add a pumpkin face to the sack using a black permanent marker, then gather the sack around the stick and tie on green curling ribbon.

Chicken Lasagna with Roasted
Red Pepper Sauce, page 52

casual get-togethers

Holiday gatherings don't have to be fancy! Invite friends & family over for a casual Christmas morning breakfast and whip up Buttermilk 'n' Honey Pancakes (page 40) while the kids open presents from Santa Claus. Easter Sunday simply wouldn't be complete without a ham…slice up Whole Baked Ham (page 59) and serve it on yummy rolls for fun finger-sandwiches. Celebrate the Fourth of July with tasty Corn Dogs (page 67)…they'll bring out the kid in everyone! Enjoy your favorite holidays throughout the year with these delicious recipes.

Buttermilk 'n' Honey Pancakes

Honey adds sweetness and moisture to these pancakes. Experiment by using dark or wildflower honey.

1 c. all-purpose flour	1 egg, lightly beaten
1 t. baking powder	1 c. buttermilk
½ t. baking soda	2 T. honey
¼ t. salt	

Stir together first 4 ingredients in a medium bowl. Add egg, buttermilk and honey, stirring until well blended.

Pour ¼ cup batter onto a hot, lightly greased griddle or skillet. Cook one to 2 minutes or until top is covered with bubbles and edges look cooked. Turn and cook one more minute. Repeat with remaining batter. Top pancakes with Pecan-Honey Butter, if desired. Serve with syrup. Makes about 9 (3-inch) pancakes.

Note: For 5 jumbo pancakes, use a heaping ⅓ cup batter for each pancake.

Pecan-Honey Butter:

Let the chilled Pecan-Honey Butter stand at room temperature 10 to 15 minutes to soften before serving.

½ c. butter, softened	2 T. honey
⅓ c. finely chopped pecans, toasted	⅛ to ¼ t. cinnamon

Stir together all ingredients until blended. Cover and chill until ready to serve. Makes about ¾ cup.

Banana Bread French Toast

Serve warm with your favorite syrup.

4 eggs, lightly beaten
1 c. milk
3 T. butter, divided

14-oz. pkg. banana bread mix
Optional: chopped pecans, sliced
   banana

Prepare and bake banana bread according to package directions; let cool and slice. Whisk together eggs and milk.

Melt 1½ tablespoons butter in a large non-stick skillet over medium-high heat. Lightly dip bread slices, one at a time, in egg mixture. Cook bread slices, in batches, 2 to 3 minutes on each side or until golden. Add remaining butter to skillet as needed.

Top each serving with pecans and sliced banana, if desired. Serve hot. Serves 4 to 5.

buttery goodness

Whip up tasty maple butter in no time...yummy on pancakes or French toast. Just combine ½ cup softened butter with ¾ cup maple syrup.

Garden-Fresh
Egg Casserole

Garden-Fresh Egg Casserole

Fresh tomatoes and spinach turn this breakfast casserole into something extra special!

18 eggs, beaten
1½ c. shredded Monterey Jack cheese
1 c. buttermilk
1 c. cottage cheese

1 c. spinach, chopped
1 c. tomatoes, chopped
½ c. butter, melted
½ c. onion, grated

It's perfect for overnight guests!

Anne

Combine all ingredients; pour into a greased 13"x9" baking pan. Cover; refrigerate overnight. Bake, uncovered, at 350 degrees for 50 minutes to one hour. Serves 8 to 10.

Anne Muns
Scottsdale, AZ

Christmas

Christmas Morning Chile Relleno

Serve with fruit salad and sausage links for a spicy Christmas breakfast.

16-oz. pkg. shredded Cheddar cheese
16-oz. pkg. shredded Monterey Jack cheese
2 (4-oz.) cans chopped green chiles

4 eggs
1 c. evaporated milk
¼ c. all-purpose flour

Sprinkle cheeses and chiles together alternately in a greased 13"x9" baking pan. Whisk together eggs, milk and flour in a medium bowl and pour over cheese mixture. Bake, uncovered, at 350 degrees for 30 minutes. Let cool slightly before serving. Serves 8 to 10.

Angela Leikem
Silverton, OR

Spicy Pasta Alfredo Casserole

Sassy ingredients…tomatoes and green chiles, artichoke hearts and roasted peppers…team up for a meatless main dish or a rich side to chicken, ham or beef.

2 (1.6-oz.) pkgs. Alfredo
    sauce mix
2 c. milk
1 c. water
2 T. butter or margarine
16-oz. container sour cream
10-oz. can diced tomatoes with
    green chiles, drained

12-oz. pkg. fettuccine, cooked
14-oz. can quartered artichoke
    hearts, drained
12-oz. jar roasted red peppers,
    drained and chopped
1 c. freshly grated or finely
    shredded refrigerated
    Parmesan cheese

Combine sauce mix and next 3 ingredients in a large saucepan; bring to a boil over medium heat, stirring constantly. Reduce heat; cook, stirring constantly, 2 minutes or until sauce is thickened and bubbly. Stir in sour cream and tomatoes.

Combine pasta, sauce mixture, artichokes and red peppers; spoon mixture into a greased 13"x9" baking pan. (If desired, cover and chill overnight. Let stand at room temperature 30 minutes before baking.)

Cover and bake at 350 degrees for one hour. Uncover and sprinkle with cheese; bake, uncovered, 10 more minutes or until lightly golden. Serves 6.

Linguine & White Clam Sauce

2 (6½-oz.) cans minced clams,
    drained and juice reserved
milk
½ c. onion, finely chopped
1 clove garlic, minced
2 T. butter
¼ c. all-purpose flour

½ t. dried oregano
½ t. salt
¼ t. pepper
¼ c. sherry or chicken broth
2 T. dried parsley
8-oz. pkg. linguine, cooked
½ c. grated Parmesan cheese

Combine reserved clam juice with enough milk to equal 2 cups liquid; set aside. In a medium saucepan, cook onion and garlic in butter over medium heat until tender and golden; stir in flour. Add clam juice mixture to saucepan; stir until smooth over low heat. Add oregano, salt and pepper; cook until thick and bubbly, stirring frequently. Stir in clams and sherry or broth; cook one more minute. Sprinkle with parsley; stir. Toss with cooked linguine; sprinkle with Parmesan cheese. Serves 4.

Kristie Rigo
Friedens, PA

Sometimes I add a teaspoon of red pepper flakes along with the oregano...my family likes a little kick!

Kristie

Garlicky Baked Shrimp

Here's the perfect party recipe…guests peel their own shrimp and save you the work!

2 lbs. uncooked large shrimp,
    rinsed and unpeeled
16-oz. bottle Italian salad
    dressing
1½ T. pepper

2 cloves garlic, pressed
2 lemons, halved
¼ c. fresh parsley, chopped
½ c. butter, cut into pieces

Place first 4 ingredients in a 13"x9" baking pan, tossing to coat. Squeeze juice from lemons over shrimp mixture and stir. Add lemon halves to pan. Sprinkle shrimp with parsley; dot with butter.

Bake, uncovered, at 375 degrees for 25 minutes, stirring after 15 minutes. Serve in pan. Serves 6.

make it easier

To bake this when you're on vacation, purchase a large disposable roasting pan for easy clean-up. French bread is perfect to sop up the savory sauce.

Herbed Shrimp Tacos

We love to make these tacos in the summer...we simply grill the shrimp on metal skewers after marinating. They're so good!

Laurie

juice of 1 lime
½ c. plus 1 T. fresh cilantro,
    chopped and divided
1 t. salt
½ t. pepper
⅛ t. dried thyme
⅛ t. dried oregano
1 lb. uncooked medium shrimp,
    peeled and cleaned
½ c. radishes, shredded
½ c. green cabbage, shredded
½ c. red onion, chopped
Optional: 2 T. oil
10 (6-inch) flour tortillas,
    warmed

Combine lime juice, one tablespoon cilantro, salt, pepper and herbs in a large plastic zipping bag; mix well. Add shrimp; seal bag and refrigerate at least 4 hours. Mix together radishes, cabbage, onion and remaining cilantro; set aside. Thread shrimp onto skewers; grill over medium-high heat until pink and cooked through or heat oil in a skillet over medium heat and sauté shrimp until done. Spoon into warm tortillas; garnish with guacamole and cabbage mixture. Serves 10.

Guacamole:

2 avocados, pitted, peeled and
    mashed
1 T. sour cream
1 T. hot pepper sauce
juice of 1 lime
1 t. garlic salt
¼ t. pepper

Combine all ingredients in a small bowl. Makes about 2 cups.

Laurie Vincent
Alpine, UT

Firecracker Grilled Salmon

4 (4- to 6-oz.) salmon fillets
¼ c. peanut oil
2 T. soy sauce
2 T. balsamic vinegar
2 T. green onions, chopped

1½ t. brown sugar, packed
1 clove garlic, minced
½ t. red pepper flakes
½ t. sesame oil
⅛ t. salt

Add more red pepper flakes or a dusting of cayenne pepper for even more heat!

Sharon

Place salmon in a glass baking pan. Whisk together remaining ingredients and pour over salmon. Cover with plastic wrap; refrigerate 4 to 6 hours. Remove salmon, discarding marinade. Place on an aluminum foil-lined grill that has been sprayed with non-stick vegetable spray. Grill 10 minutes per inch of thickness, measured at thickest part, until fish flakes easily with a fork. Turn halfway through cooking. Serves 4.

Sharon Demers
Dolores, CO

a special touch

When serving seafood, wrap lemon halves in cheesecloth, tie with colorful ribbon and set one on each plate. Guests can squeeze the lemon over their food…the cheesecloth prevents squirting and catches seeds!

Divine Chicken & Wild Rice Casserole

Perfect for a big family get-together, it feeds a crowd. You can make and freeze the casserole ahead or make 2 smaller casseroles.

2 (6.2-oz.) pkgs. fast-cooking long-grain and wild rice mix

¼ c. butter

4 stalks celery, chopped

2 onions, chopped

2 (8-oz.) cans sliced water chestnuts, drained

5 c. cooked chicken, chopped

4 c. shredded Cheddar cheese, divided

2 (10¾-oz.) cans cream of mushroom soup

2 (8-oz.) containers sour cream

1 c. milk

½ t. salt

½ t. pepper

2 c. soft bread crumbs

2¼-oz. pkg. sliced almonds, toasted

Prepare rice mixes according to package directions.

Melt butter in a large skillet over medium heat; add celery and onion. Sauté 10 minutes or until tender. Stir in rice, water chestnuts, chicken, 3 cups cheese and next 5 ingredients.

Spoon mixture into a lightly greased 4-quart casserole dish. Top with bread crumbs.

Bake, uncovered, at 350 degrees for 35 minutes. Sprinkle with remaining one cup cheese and almonds; bake 5 more minutes. Serves 10 to 12.

Note: You can divide this casserole evenly between 2 (13"x9") baking pans. They'll just be slightly shallow as opposed to brimming over. Bake as directed above or freeze casseroles up to one month. Remove from freezer and let stand at room temperature one hour. Bake, covered, at 350 degrees for 30 minutes. Uncover and bake 55 more minutes. Sprinkle with remaining one cup cheese and almonds; bake 5 more minutes.

Chicken Lasagna with Roasted Red Pepper Sauce

(pictured on page 38)

There's nothing like a hot pan of lasagna on a cold winter's night!

Jo Ann

4 c. cooked chicken, finely chopped
2 (8-oz.) containers chive-and-onion cream cheese
10-oz. pkg. frozen chopped spinach, thawed and well drained

1 t. seasoned pepper
¾ t. garlic salt
9 no-boil lasagna noodles
2 c. shredded Italian 3-cheese blend

Stir together first 5 ingredients.

Layer a lightly greased 11"x7" baking pan with ⅓ of Roasted Red Pepper Sauce, 3 noodles, ⅓ of chicken mixture and ⅓ of cheese. Repeat layers twice. Place baking pan on a baking sheet.

Bake, covered, at 350 degrees for 50 to 55 minutes or until thoroughly heated. Uncover and bake 15 more minutes. Serves 6 to 8.

Roasted Red Pepper Sauce:

This sauce is also great over your favorite noodles!

12-oz. jar roasted red peppers, drained
16-oz. jar creamy Alfredo sauce

¾ c. grated Parmesan cheese
½ t. red pepper flakes

Process all ingredients in a food processor until smooth, stopping to scrape down sides. Makes 3½ cups.

Jo Ann
Gooseberry Patch

Fabulous Fajitas

Make-ahead simplicity and delicious taste make these fajitas a family favorite. To warm tortillas, wrap them in aluminum foil and bake at 325 degrees for 15 minutes or until thoroughly heated.

1 lb. boneless, skinless chicken
    breasts, cut into strips
2 T. cornstarch
2 T. lemon juice
1 t. garlic powder
1 t. seasoned salt
½ t. dried oregano
½ t. pepper
⅛ t. smoke-flavored cooking
    sauce

2 T. oil
1 green pepper, cut into strips
1 onion, halved and thinly sliced
1 tomato, cut into thin wedges
½ c. salsa
8 (8-inch) flour tortillas, warmed
Garnish: salsa, sour cream

Combine first 8 ingredients in a medium bowl or heavy-duty plastic zipping bag. Cover or seal; marinate at least 2 hours or up to 24 hours. Remove chicken and discard marinade.

Sauté chicken in oil in a large skillet for 6 minutes or until done. Add green pepper and onion; cook 4 minutes or until crisp-tender. Add tomato and salsa; simmer one to 2 minutes or until thoroughly heated. Divide mixture evenly among tortillas. Roll up tortillas; top each serving with additional salsa and sour cream. Serve immediately. Serves 8.

quick table setting

You don't have to spend a lot of time setting the table for casual gatherings. Just wrap colorful napkins around silverware and slip one bundle into a glass at each place setting. It's so charming…and you don't have to remember where the forks, knives and spoons go!

Grilled Chicken with White BBQ Sauce

Aromatic herbs scent the air when you grill this chicken seasoned with a dry rub. The flavors go well with a creamy white barbecue sauce spiced with tangy brown mustard and a spoonful of horseradish.

3 lbs. chicken thighs and
    drumsticks
1 T. dried thyme
1 T. dried oregano
1 T. ground cumin

1 T. paprika
1 t. onion powder
½ t. salt
½ t. pepper

Rinse chicken and pat dry with paper towels. Combine remaining ingredients; rub mixture evenly over chicken. Place chicken in a large plastic zipping bag. Seal and chill 4 hours.

Remove chicken from bag, discarding bag. Grill, covered with grill lid, over medium-high heat (350 to 400 degrees) for 8 to 10 minutes on each side or until a meat thermometer inserted into thickest portion registers 165 degrees or to desired doneness. Serve with White BBQ Sauce. Serves 5.

White BBQ Sauce:

1½ c. mayonnaise
¼ c. white wine vinegar
1 clove garlic, minced
1 T. coarsely ground pepper

1 T. spicy brown mustard
1 t. sugar
1 t. salt
2 t. horseradish

Stir together all ingredients until well blended. Store in an airtight container in refrigerator at least 2 hours and up to one week. Makes 1¾ cups.

Honey-Glazed Turkey Breast

¼ c. honey

1 T. Dijon mustard

1 T. Worcestershire sauce

1 T. butter or margarine, melted

3-lb. boneless turkey breast

1 T. oil

1 t. salt

½ t. pepper

Stir together first 4 ingredients; set aside.

Rinse turkey breast and pat dry with paper towels; brush with oil. Place in a shallow roasting pan. Sprinkle turkey breast with salt and pepper. Baste turkey breast with honey mixture.

Roast turkey breast at 325 degrees for one hour and 25 minutes or until a meat thermometer inserted in turkey breast registers 170 degrees. Baste with honey glaze during the last 25 minutes of baking. Transfer turkey to a platter and let stand 15 minutes before slicing. Serves 6.

Adrienne Payne
Omaha, NE

Deep-Fried Turkey

*Fried turkey is incredibly moist, succulent and amazingly has
no greasy taste!*

12- to 15-lb. turkey
Optional: 2 T. cayenne pepper
4 to 5 gal. peanut oil

Optional: fresh sage, parsley
and thyme sprigs, kumquats
with leaves

Remove giblets and neck; rinse turkey with cold water. Drain cavity
well; pat dry. Place turkey on fryer rod; allow all liquid to drain from
cavity (20 to 30 minutes). Rub outside of turkey with cayenne pepper,
if desired.

Pour oil into a deep propane turkey fryer 10 to 12 inches from
top; heat to 375 degrees over a medium-low flame according to
manufacturer's instructions. Carefully lower turkey into hot oil
with rod attachment.

Fry 55 minutes or until a meat thermometer inserted in turkey
breast registers 165 degrees or to desired doneness. (Keep oil temperature
at 340 degrees.) Remove turkey from oil; drain and let stand 15 minutes
before slicing. Garnish with fresh sage, parsley and thyme sprigs and
kumquats, if desired. Serves 20.

kids' table

Make the kids' table fun! Use a sheet of butcher paper for the
tablecloth; place a flowerpot filled with markers, crayons and
stickers in the middle...they'll have a blast!

Whole Baked Ham

A yummy ham that can be served hot or refrigerated and sliced for sandwiches.

12- to 14-lb. fully cooked
    boneless or bone-in ham
12 whole cloves
1½ c. pineapple juice
½ c. maple-flavored syrup

6 slices canned pineapple
1 c. water
¾ c. brown sugar, packed
3 T. mustard

Place ham, fat side up, in a shallow roasting pan. Press cloves into top of ham. Stir together pineapple juice and syrup; pour over ham. Arrange pineapple slices on ham. Bake at 325 degrees for 1½ hours. Add water and bake 1½ more hours. Remove from oven; remove pineapple slices. Mix together brown sugar and mustard; spread over ham. Bake 30 more minutes. Serves 18 to 20.

Jacqueline Kurtz
Reading, PA

Chunky Ham Pot Pie

Feed your family this pot pie brimming with ham, veggies and Cheddar cheese.

1 lb. new potatoes, coarsely chopped
10-oz. pkg. frozen cut broccoli or flowerets
2 T. butter or margarine
1 c. onion, chopped
10¾-oz. can cream of potato soup, undiluted
8-oz. container sour cream

1 c. shredded sharp Cheddar cheese
¾ c. milk
½ t. garlic powder
½ t. salt
¼ t. pepper
2½ c. cooked ham, chopped
9-inch pie crust

Cook potatoes in boiling water to cover 10 minutes or until barely tender; drain. Meanwhile, cook broccoli according to package directions; drain.

Melt butter in a large skillet over medium heat; add onion. Cook 10 minutes or until onion is tender and begins to brown, stirring often.

Combine soup and next 6 ingredients in a large bowl, stirring well. Stir in onion, potatoes, broccoli and ham. Spoon ham mixture into a greased 3½-quart casserole dish. (If desired, cover and chill overnight. Let stand at room temperature 30 minutes before baking.)

Unfold pie crust onto a lightly floured surface. Roll out to extend ¾ inch beyond edges of casserole dish. Place pastry over ham mixture. Seal edges and crimp. Cut slits in top of pastry to allow steam to escape. Bake, uncovered, at 400 degrees for 45 minutes or until golden. Let stand 10 minutes before serving. Serves 6 to 8.

Note: You can divide this pot pie into two 2-quart dishes. Bake one now and freeze one for later. You will need 2 pie crusts for 2 casseroles. Top the casserole to be frozen with crust before freezing, but do not cut slits in top until ready to bake. Let frozen casserole stand at room temperature 20 minutes before baking.

Hearty Black-Eyed Peas

Serve these slow-simmered peas plain or with rice and cornbread.

3 c. water
3 c. low-sodium chicken broth
1 onion, chopped
1 smoked ham hock
1 bay leaf
½ t. pepper

Optional: 4 whole jalapeño
    peppers
16-oz. pkg. dried black-eyed
    peas
1 t. salt, divided

Bring water, broth, next 4 ingredients and, if desired, jalapeños to a boil in a Dutch oven; cover, reduce heat and simmer 30 minutes.

Rinse and sort peas according to package directions. Add peas and ½ teaspoon salt to Dutch oven; cook, covered, one hour or until peas are tender. If desired, remove meat from ham hock, finely chop and return to Dutch oven. Season with remaining salt. Remove and discard bay leaf. Serves 4 to 6.

lucky year

Good luck is said to be the reward for eating black-eyed peas on New Year's Day. Try this tasty recipe to bring your family good fortune!

Red Beans & Rice

This recipe takes a shortcut by using canned beans in place of dried.
Kick it up a notch by using andouille sausage and shaking a few drops
of hot sauce on top!

1 lb. Kielbasa sausage, cut into
    ¼-inch slices
1 onion, chopped
1 green pepper, chopped
1 clove garlic, minced
2 (16-oz.) cans dark kidney
    beans, drained

14½-oz. can diced tomatoes
½ t. dried oregano
½ t. pepper
4 c. hot cooked rice

Cook sausage in a Dutch oven over low heat 6 minutes, stirring often. Add onion, green pepper and garlic; cook over medium-high heat 5 minutes or until tender. Add beans, tomtatoes, oregano and pepper; reduce heat and simmer, uncovered, 20 minutes, stirring occasionally. Serve over rice. Serves 4 to 6.

Vickie
Gooseberry Patch

We love the
flavor and simplicity
of this version
of the traditional
New Orleans dish.

Vickie

Christmas Breakfast Stratas

These casseroles can be partially made ahead and assembled just before baking. Cook the sausage a day ahead and store in a plastic zipping bag in the refrigerator. The bread can also be cubed a day ahead and stored at room temperature in a plastic zipping bag. These casseroles can also be made in two 11"x7" baking pans.

2 (1-lb.) pkgs. hot ground pork sausage

16-oz. loaf sliced French bread, cut into 1-inch cubes

4 c. shredded Cheddar and Monterey Jack cheese blend, divided

8-oz. pkg. sliced mushrooms, coarsely chopped

4½-oz. can diced green chiles, drained

4-oz. can sliced ripe olives, drained

8 eggs, lightly beaten

4 c. milk

1 t. salt

1 t. onion powder

1 t. dry mustard

1 t. dried oregano

¼ t. pepper

Optional: sour cream, salsa

Cook sausage in a large skillet over medium-high heat, stirring until it crumbles and is no longer pink. Drain and set aside.

Divide bread cubes between a lightly greased 13"x9" baking pan and an 8"x8" baking pan. Divide 2 cups cheese over bread cubes. Sprinkle with cooked sausage, mushrooms, green chiles and olives.

Whisk together eggs and next 6 ingredients in a medium bowl. Pour mixture over casseroles. Sprinkle with remaining cheese. Bake, uncovered, at 350 degrees for one hour or until set. Garnish with sour cream and salsa, if desired. Serves 20.

casual Christmas breakfast

Start off Christmas Day with some family fun! Get the family involved in making biscuits from scratch. Start a bowl of fruit salad the night before and do the prep work for Christmas Breakfast Stratas. While the biscuits bake, let the coffee perk and the children peek in their stockings.

Pork Chops & Rice Skillet

4 (1-inch-thick) pork chops
1 t. salt, divided
½ t. pepper, divided
¼ t. garlic powder
2 T. oil
1¼ c. water

¾ c. long-grain rice, uncooked
¾ c. onion, chopped
15¼-oz. can corn, drained
14½-oz. can diced tomatoes,
    drained

Sprinkle pork chops evenly with ½ teaspoon salt, ¼ teaspoon pepper and garlic powder. Heat oil in a large skillet over medium-high heat; add pork chops. Cook 2 to 3 minutes on each side or until golden. Remove pork chops and set aside.

Add water, rice, onion and remaining ½ teaspoon salt to skillet; stir to combine. Place pork chops on top of rice mixture. Top rice and pork chops evenly with corn and tomatoes. Sprinkle with remaining ¼ teaspoon pepper. Bring to a boil; reduce heat, cover and simmer 20 to 25 minutes or until rice is tender and pork chops are done. Let stand 5 minutes before serving. Serves 4.

Corn Dogs

1 c. all-purpose flour
2 T. sugar
1½ t. baking powder
1 t. salt
⅔ c. cornmeal
2 T. shortening

1 egg
¾ c. milk
8 to 10 hot dogs
8 to 10 wooden sticks
oil for deep frying

Combine flour, sugar, baking powder and salt; stir in cornmeal. Using a pastry cutter or 2 forks, cut in shortening until coarse crumbs form; set aside. Blend together egg and milk in a separate bowl. Stir into cornmeal mixture. Thoroughly dry each hot dog with a paper towel to ensure batter will cling. Insert a stick into each; dip in batter. Deep-fry in 350- to 375-degree oil 4 to 5 minutes or until golden. Serves 8 to 10.

Kay Marone
Des Moines, IA

a fun twist!

Give Corn Dogs a new spin by using Italian sausage or bratwurst instead of hot dogs.

Tried & True Meatloaf

Thanks to the slow cooker, this recipe is so easy to make!

1½ lbs. ground beef
¾ c. bread crumbs
2 eggs
¾ c. milk
1 onion, chopped
1 t. salt

¼ t. pepper
¼ c. catsup
2 T. brown sugar, packed
1 t. dry mustard
¼ t. nutmeg

Combine beef, bread crumbs, eggs, milk, onion, salt and pepper in a bowl; form mixture into a loaf. Place in a 3-quart oval slow cooker; cover and cook on high setting one hour. Reduce heat to low setting and cook 4 to 5 hours. Whisk together remaining ingredients; pour over beef. Cover and cook on high setting 15 more minutes. Serves 4 to 6.

Jo Ann
Gooseberry Patch

meatloaf sandwiches

Cut meatloaf into thin slices, wrap individually and freeze. Later, they can be thawed and rewarmed quickly for scrumptious meatloaf sandwiches at a few moments' notice.

Bacon-Wrapped Burgers

3 lbs. ground beef
¾ c. onion, finely chopped
2 T. Greek seasoning
24 slices bacon
12 onion rolls, split

Chunky Guacamole (see recipe
   on page 31)
Garnish: assorted cheeses,
   commercial salsa, catsup or
   other toppings

Combine ground beef, onion and Greek seasoning; shape into
12 patties.

Place 2 slices of bacon in a crisscross pattern on a flat surface. Place a
patty in center of bacon; pull bacon around patty and tie ends of bacon
in a loose knot. Repeat with remaining bacon and patties.

Grill hamburgers, uncovered, over medium-high heat (350 to 400
degrees) 6 minutes on each side or to desired degree of doneness. Serve
on rolls with Chunky Guacamole, assorted cheeses, commercial salsa,
catsup or other toppings. Serves 12.

Ultimate Cheeseburger Pizza

To avoid having to get out the cutting board, use kitchen shears to chop tomatoes while they are still in the can.

½ lb. lean ground beef
14½-oz. can whole tomatoes,
   drained and chopped
1 t. bottled minced garlic

12-inch prebaked pizza crust
1½ c. shredded Cheddar cheese
¼ c. green onions, chopped
½ t. salt

Brown beef in a skillet over medium-high heat, stirring often, 4 minutes or until beef crumbles and is no longer pink; drain well.

Stir together tomatoes and garlic. Spread crust evenly with tomato mixture; sprinkle with ground beef, cheese, green onions and salt.

Bake at 450 degrees directly on oven rack for 12 to 14 minutes or until cheese is melted. Serves 4.

kitchen journal

Jot down favorite recipes and family members' preferences in a kitchen journal. It'll make meal planning a snap!

Creamy Beef Stroganoff

With this dish in the freezer, you and your family will be able to enjoy a great, easy meal during the holidays.

1½ lbs. sirloin steak
2 T. oil
1½ c. sliced mushrooms
½ c. onion, chopped
1 clove garlic, minced
½ c. dry sherry or beef broth
½ c. beef broth
1 T. lemon zest

1 t. dried chervil
1 t. dried parsley
½ t. salt
pepper to taste
3-oz. pkg. cream cheese
1 c. sour cream
hot cooked noodles or rice

Partially freeze steak; slice diagonally across grain into ¼-inch strips. Brown meat in hot oil in a large skillet; remove meat from skillet, reserving pan drippings. Sauté mushrooms, onions and garlic in reserved pan drippings until tender.

Return steak to skillet; add sherry or broth, ½ cup beef broth and next 5 ingredients. Cook over medium-low heat 10 to 12 minutes or until most of liquid evaporates. Remove from heat; add cream cheese, stirring until cheese melts. Cool.

To Store: Refrigerate beef mixture in a tightly covered container up to 2 days. Freeze mixture in an airtight container up to 2 weeks.

To Serve: Thaw in refrigerator. Cook in a large saucepan over medium heat until simmering, stirring frequently. Stir in sour cream; cook just until hot. (Do not boil.) Serve stroganoff over noodles or rice. Serves 4 to 6.

Hickory-Smoked Kabobs

1½ lbs. top sirloin steak, cut into
    1½-inch cubes
8-oz. bottle Russian salad
    dressing
¼ c. hickory-smoked
    Worcestershire sauce
1 t. smoke-flavored cooking
    sauce
½ t. pepper

3 onions
12 mushrooms
1 green pepper, cut into 1½-inch
    pieces
1 red pepper, cut into 1½-inch
    pieces
3 lemons, cut into wedges
6 (14-inch) skewers

Place meat in a shallow dish. Combine dressing and next
3 ingredients; stir well. Pour mixture over meat. Cover and marinate
in refrigerator 8 hours; stir occasionally.

Cook onions in boiling water to cover 2 minutes. Drain and cut
onions into quarters.

Remove meat from marinade, reserving marinade. Bring reserved
marinade to a boil. Alternate meat, onion, mushrooms, pepper pieces
and lemon wedges on skewers. Grill, covered, over medium-high heat
(350 to 400 degrees) 6 minutes on each side or to desired degree of
doneness, basting frequently with reserved marinade. Squeeze lemon
wedges over kabobs before serving, if desired. Serves 6.

Roast Turkey & Gravy, page 92
Cornbread Dressing, page 156

memorable main dishes

Every holiday meal needs a main dish! If you're searching

for that perfect dish for a summertime soiree, Mother's Fried

Chicken (page 87) is sure to satisfy partygoers

of all ages. For the big holiday feast, serve a

classic...Roast Turkey & Gravy (page 92)

with a side of creamy mashed potatoes.

On Valentine's Day, enjoy Tenderloin for

Two with Peppercorn Cream (page 108).

Check out these and other scrumptious recipes

in this chapter to fit your special occasion.

Cheese & Chile Casserole

*Punch up the heat in this ultra-rich brunch dish by using
Pepper Jack cheese.*

9 eggs
¾ t. salt
3 (8-oz.) pkgs. Monterey Jack
  cheese, cubed
2 (8-oz.) pkgs. cream cheese,
  cubed
12-oz. container small-curd
  cottage cheese

1 T. butter or margarine, cut into
  small pieces
¾ c. all-purpose flour
1½ t. baking powder
4½-oz. can chopped green
  chiles, drained
2-oz. jar diced pimento, drained

Whisk together eggs and salt in a large bowl; add cheeses and butter. Whisk flour and baking powder into cheese mixture. Add green chiles and pimento. Pour into a lightly greased 13"x9" baking pan.

Bake, uncovered, at 350 degrees for 45 minutes or until set. Let stand 10 to 15 minutes before serving. Serves 16.

Shiitake Mushroom & Spinach Manicotti

12 manicotti or cannelloni shells
⅓ plus ¼ c. butter or margarine, divided
4½ c. sliced shiitake or other mushrooms
2 cloves garlic, minced
10-oz. pkg. fresh spinach, coarse stems removed
1 c. ricotta cheese
¾ c. grated Parmesan cheese
1 egg, beaten
½ t. salt
½ t. pepper
2 T. all-purpose flour
2 c. half-and-half
½ t. salt
1 c. shredded Gouda cheese
2 slices 7-grain sandwich bread
1½ c. shredded Mexican 4-cheese blend
3 T. butter or margarine, melted

Cook shells according to package directions; drain.

Meanwhile, melt 3 tablespoons butter in a large skillet; add mushrooms and garlic and sauté until mushroom liquid is absorbed. Transfer mushroom mixture to a large bowl.

Melt remaining one tablespoon butter in skillet. Add spinach; cover and cook over medium-low heat 5 minutes or until spinach wilts. Add spinach to mushroom mixture. Stir in ricotta cheese and next 4 ingredients. Spoon spinach mixture evenly into cooked shells. Place stuffed shells in a greased 13"x9" baking pan.

Melt ⅓ cup butter in a heavy saucepan over low heat; whisk in flour until smooth. Cook one minute, whisking constantly. Gradually whisk in half-and-half; cook over medium heat, whisking constantly, until mixture is thickened and bubbly. Stir in ½ teaspoon salt. Add Gouda cheese, stirring until cheese melts. Pour over stuffed shells.

Process bread in a blender or food processor until it resembles coarse crumbs. Spread crumbs in a small pan; bake at 350 degrees for 3 to 4 minutes or until toasted.

Combine toasted crumbs, cheese blend and 3 tablespoons melted butter in a bowl; toss well and sprinkle over shells. Bake, uncovered, at 350 degrees for 45 minutes or until bubbly. Serves 6.

Laurie's Stuffed Peppers

4 green, red or yellow peppers
2 T. olive oil
8-oz. pkg. mushrooms, finely
    chopped
1 onion, finely chopped
1 clove garlic, pressed
1 c. white rice, cooked

1 c. brown rice, cooked
3 to 4 dashes hot pepper sauce
salt and pepper to taste
2 (15-oz.) cans tomato sauce,
    divided
1 c. shredded mozzarella cheese
Optional: fresh thyme sprigs

For this recipe, I like to use red, yellow and orange peppers for a colorful, summertime look and sweeter taste.

Laurie

Slice off tops of peppers; remove seeds. Fill a large soup pot with water; bring water to a boil over medium-high heat. Add peppers; boil 5 minutes. Remove peppers; set aside. Heat oil in a large skillet over medium heat; add mushrooms, onion and garlic. Sauté 5 minutes or until onion is tender. Add white rice, brown rice, hot sauce, salt and pepper; cook 2 minutes. Add one can tomato sauce and simmer 5 minutes; spoon into peppers. Spread half can tomato sauce into an ungreased 13"x9" baking pan. Place peppers in pan; pour remaining sauce over top. Bake, uncovered, at 350 degrees for 25 minutes; sprinkle with cheese. Bake an additional 10 minutes or until cheese is melted. Garnish with thyme sprigs, if desired. Serves 4.

Laurie Patton
Pinckney, MI

simple seasonings

Use dried herbs from the herb garden to make a terrific seasoning blend. Combine one cup sea salt with 2 tablespoons each of rosemary, thyme, lemon balm, mint, tarragon, dill weed and paprika. Stir in 4 tablespoons parsley and basil. Blend, in batches, in a food processor, and store in a glass shaker.

Almond-and-Herb-Crusted Trout

⅔ c. saltine cracker crumbs

⅓ c. almonds, ground

3 T. fresh thyme, chopped

½ t. pepper

2 lbs. trout fillets

½ c. milk

⅔ c. oil

Optional: fresh thyme sprigs

Combine cracker crumbs, ground almonds, thyme and pepper in a shallow bowl; stir well. Dip trout fillets in milk. Dredge fillets in cracker crumb mixture.

Pan-fry fillets, a few at a time, in hot oil in a large heavy skillet 3 minutes on each side or until golden. Drain on paper towels. Garnish, if desired. Serves 8.

side dish time-saver

Purchase prepared mashed potatoes at the grocery store. Heat up, blend in sour cream and cream cheese to taste, then heat up again and stir until well blended...so yummy!

Rich Seafood Casserole

Fresh shrimp and scallops come to the table baked in a Swiss cheese and wine sauce that you can spoon over hot cooked rice. This dish can be made the day before. After assembling the casserole, cover and chill overnight. Let stand at room temperature 30 minutes before baking.

1½ c. dry white wine or chicken broth
¼ c. onion, chopped
¼ c. fresh parsley sprigs or celery leaves
1 T. butter or margarine
1 t. salt
1½ lbs. large shrimp, cleaned
1 lb. bay scallops
3 T. butter or margarine
3 T. all-purpose flour
1 c. half-and-half

½ c. shredded Swiss cheese
1 T. lemon juice
¾ t. lemon-pepper seasoning
7-oz. can sliced mushrooms, drained
1 c. soft whole-wheat bread crumbs
¼ c. grated Parmesan cheese
¼ c. sliced almonds
2 T. butter or margarine, melted
hot cooked rice

Combine wine or broth and next 4 ingredients in a Dutch oven; bring to a boil. Add shrimp and scallops; cook 3 to 5 minutes or until shrimp turn pink. Drain shrimp mixture, reserving ⅔ cup broth.

Melt 3 tablespoons butter in Dutch oven over low heat; add flour, stirring until smooth. Cook, stirring constantly, one minute. Gradually add half-and-half; cook over medium heat, stirring constantly, until mixture is thickened and bubbly. Add Swiss cheese, stirring until cheese melts. Gradually stir in reserved ⅔ cup broth, lemon juice and lemon-pepper seasoning. Stir in shrimp mixture and mushrooms.

Spoon mixture into a lightly greased 11"x7" baking pan. Cover and bake at 350 degrees for 40 minutes. Combine bread crumbs and next 3 ingredients; sprinkle over casserole. Bake, uncovered, 10 minutes. Let stand 10 minutes before serving. Serve over rice. Serves 8.

Party Paella Casserole

Here's a great use for rotisserie chicken, shrimp and yellow rice.

2 (8-oz.) pkgs. yellow rice
1 lb. medium shrimp, cleaned
1 T. fresh lemon juice
½ t. salt
¼ t. pepper
2 cloves garlic, minced
1½ T. olive oil
2½-lb. lemon-and-garlic
    deli-roasted whole chicken,
    coarsely shredded

5 green onions, chopped
8-oz. container sour cream
1 c. frozen English peas, thawed
1 c. green olives with pimentos,
    coarsely chopped
1½ c. shredded Monterey Jack
    cheese
½ t. smoked Spanish paprika

Prepare rice according to package directions. Remove from heat and let cool 30 minutes; fluff with a fork.

Meanwhile, toss shrimp with lemon juice, salt and pepper in a bowl. Sauté seasoned shrimp and garlic in hot oil in a large non-stick skillet 2 minutes or just until done. Remove from heat.

Combine shredded chicken, rice, green onions, sour cream and peas in a large bowl; toss well. Add shrimp and olives, tossing gently. Spoon rice mixture into a greased 13"x9" baking pan.

Combine cheese and paprika, tossing well; sprinkle over casserole.

Bake, uncovered, at 400 degrees for 15 minutes or just until cheese is melted and casserole is thoroughly heated. Serves 8.

Creamy Chicken à la King

This hearty dish can also be served over rice, mashed potatoes or hot biscuits.

1 c. sliced mushrooms
5 T. butter or margarine, divided
½ red pepper, diced
¾ c. fresh or frozen peas
¼ c. all-purpose flour
32-oz. container chicken broth

3 c. cooked chicken, cubed
½ c. sliced cooked carrots
1 T. fresh parsley, minced
salt and pepper to taste
8 oz. wide egg noodles, cooked
   and buttered

Sauté mushrooms in one tablespoon butter until tender; set aside.

Cook red pepper and peas in a small saucepan of boiling water to cover 2 minutes; rinse in cold water.

Melt remaining 4 tablespoons butter in a large saucepan; add flour, whisking 2 minutes or until smooth. Slowly add chicken broth, whisking thoroughly; simmer about 5 minutes or until thickened. Add chicken, carrots, mushrooms, red pepper, peas, parsley and seasonings. Simmer 5 more minutes, thinning with additional chicken broth or water, if necessary. Serve over hot buttered noodles. Serves 4.

Maple Roast Chicken & Veggies

1 winter squash, peeled and
    chopped
3 to 4 parsnips, peeled and
    chopped
2 stalks celery, chopped
2 carrots, chopped
1 onion, chopped
1 sweet potato, peeled and
    chopped

6- to 7-lb. whole chicken
2 T. butter or margarine, melted
½ t. salt
¼ t. pepper
½ t. dried rosemary
½ c. maple syrup

A tender, juicy chicken with sweet vegetables

Jo Ann

Spread vegetables evenly in a lightly greased roasting pan; place chicken on top. Brush chicken with butter; sprinkle with salt, pepper and rosemary. Place on lowest rack in oven and bake at 400 degrees for 1½ to 2 hours or until a meat thermometer inserted in thigh registers 180 degrees. Baste about every 10 minutes with maple syrup and pan drippings. Remove from oven and let stand 10 minutes before slicing. Serves 4 to 6.

Jo Ann
Gooseberry Patch

Mother's Fried Chicken

4 c. self-rising flour
2 T. salt
2 T. coarsely ground pepper

8 lbs. chicken
4 to 5 c. shortening, divided

Combine flour, salt and pepper in a shallow pan. Dredge chicken in flour mixture. In a large cast-iron skillet over medium-high heat, heat 3 cups shortening to 350 degrees. Working in batches, fry chicken, covered, about 10 minutes. Reduce heat to medium-low; fry 30 minutes per side. Add shortening as needed. Uncover during last 5 minutes of cooking time. Drain on paper towels. Serves 8.

Evelyn Russell
Dallas, TX

This recipe was given to me by my mother 30 years ago. It is always asked for when I cook for church get-togethers and Sunday dinners. The first time I made this for my pastor and his wife, it brought back memories for them of their mothers' fried chicken.

Evelyn

plan a picnic

A wheelbarrow or wagon is just right for holding paper plates and cups along with flatware and napkins. It's easy to take right to the picnic spot and keeps picnic tables free for holding all the scrumptious food!

Chicken Pot Pie

Use a muffin
tin to make
mini pot pies.
So quick
and easy!

Vickie

½ c. plus 2 T. butter, divided
½ c. all-purpose flour
1½ c. chicken broth
1½ c. half-and-half
¾ t. salt
½ t. pepper
8-oz. pkg. sliced mushrooms
salt and pepper to taste
1 onion, chopped

1 c. frozen green peas
3½ c. cooked chicken, hard-cooked, peeled and chopped
2 eggs, chopped
15-oz. pkg. refrigerated pie crusts
1 T. whipping cream
1 egg, lightly beaten

Melt ½ cup butter in a heavy saucepan over low heat; whisk in flour, until smooth. Cook, whisking constantly, one minute. Gradually add chicken broth and half-and-half; cook over medium heat, stirring constantly, until thickened and bubbly. Stir in ¾ teaspoon salt and ½ teaspoon pepper; set white sauce aside.

Melt one tablespoon butter in a large skillet over medium-high heat. Add mushrooms; season lightly with salt and pepper and sauté 10 minutes or until nicely browned. Don't overstir. Add mushrooms to white sauce. Add remaining one tablespoon butter to skillet. Add onion; sauté until tender. Stir in peas. Add vegetable mixture, chicken and chopped eggs to white sauce.

Fit one pie crust into a 9-inch deep-dish pie plate according to package directions. Spoon filling into crust; top with remaining pie crust. Trim off excess pastry. Fold edges under and flute. Cut slits in top. Combine cream and egg; brush over pie. Bake at 375 degrees for 30 to 40 minutes or until golden and bubbly. Serves 6.

Note: To make individual pot pies, spoon filling into 6 lightly greased one-cup baking dishes. Cut out 6 circles of pie crust dough slightly larger than diameter of baking dishes. Top each dish with a round of dough; fold edges under and flute. Cut slits in tops. Brush with egg wash. Bake at 375 degrees for 30 to 35 minutes or until golden and bubbly.

Vickie
Gooseberry Patch

Turkey & Wild Rice Casserole

Make this before the holidays and prepare it again with the turkey left after Christmas dinner.

6.2-oz. pkg. long-grain and
    wild rice mix
½ lb. ground pork sausage
1 c. sliced mushrooms
½ c. celery, sliced

1 T. cornstarch
1 c. milk
1 T. Worcestershire sauce
3 c. cooked turkey, chopped
1 c. sweetened dried cranberries

Prepare rice mix according to package directions and set aside.

Cook sausage, mushrooms and celery in a large skillet until sausage is browned, stirring to crumble meat. Drain sausage mixture, reserving one tablespoon drippings in skillet. Set sausage mixture aside.

Add cornstarch to drippings in skillet, stirring until smooth. Cook one minute, stirring constantly. Gradually add milk and Worcestershire sauce; cook over medium heat, stirring constantly, until mixture is thickened.

Combine rice, sausage mixture, sauce, turkey and cranberries. Spoon mixture into a lightly greased 11"x7" baking pan. Bake, uncovered, at 375 degrees for 40 to 45 minutes. Serves 6 to 8.

favorite recipes

Copy tried & true recipes onto file cards and have them laminated at a copying store. Punch a hole in the upper left corner and thread cards onto a key ring…now you can hang them on the fridge and they'll always be handy.

Sweet-and-Spicy Glazed Turkey

Red pepper flakes kick up the brown sugar-orange glaze that coats this turkey.

1 c. orange juice
¼ c. brown sugar, packed
2 T. butter
1 t. red pepper flakes
1 t. orange zest
¼ t. salt
¼ t. pepper
9- to 10-lb. turkey

1 orange, cut into 4 wedges
1 onion, cut into 4 wedges
2 T. butter, softened
1 t. salt
½ t. pepper
Optional: roasted Brussels
   sprouts

Combine first 7 ingredients in a medium saucepan; bring to a boil over medium-high heat. Reduce heat and simmer 15 minutes or until mixture is syrupy and reduced to about ⅔ cup. Set aside.

Remove giblets and neck from turkey; discard or refrigerate for another use. Rinse turkey with cold water; pat dry with paper towels. Place turkey, breast side up, on a lightly greased rack in an aluminum foil-lined broiler pan. Lift wingtips up and over back and tuck under bird.

Place orange and onion wedges inside turkey cavity. Rub softened butter all over outside of turkey, including legs. Tie ends of legs together with heavy string. Sprinkle turkey all over with salt and black pepper.

Bake, uncovered, at 325 degrees for one hour. Brush turkey with half of the glaze; bake, brushing with glaze every 30 minutes, 1½ more hours or until a meat thermometer inserted into meaty part of thigh registers 170 degrees. Cover turkey with aluminum foil during cooking, if necessary, to prevent excessive browning.

Transfer turkey to a serving platter; cover turkey with foil and let stand up to 30 minutes before carving. Garnish with roasted Brussels sprouts, if desired. Serves 9 to 10.

Roast Turkey & Gravy

(pictured on page 74)

12- to 14-lb. turkey
1 T. salt, divided
2 t. pepper, divided
½ c. butter, softened
1 Golden Delicious apple, quartered
1 yellow onion, quartered

2 carrots, cut into 3-inch pieces
3 stalks celery with leaves, cut into 3-inch pieces
4 c. hot water
⅓ c. all-purpose flour
Cornbread Dressing (page 156)

Remove giblets and neck from turkey; rinse and reserve for another use. Rinse turkey with cold water and pat dry. Sprinkle cavity with ½ tablespoon salt and one teaspoon pepper. Rub skin of turkey with butter; sprinkle with remaining ½ tablespoon salt and one teaspoon pepper.

Place apple, onion, carrot and celery in turkey cavity. Lift wingtips up and over back and tuck under bird. Place turkey, breast side up, on a lightly greased rack in a roasting pan. Tie ends of legs together with heavy string.

Bake at 425 degrees on lower oven rack 20 minutes. Reduce oven temperature to 325 degrees. Add hot water to pan; bake 2 to 2½ hours or until a meat thermometer inserted in turkey thigh registers 170 degrees, shielding turkey with aluminum foil after one hour and basting with pan juices every 20 minutes. Let stand 15 minutes. Transfer to a serving platter; reserve 2½ cups drippings.

Whisk together drippings and flour in a medium saucepan. Cook over medium heat, whisking constantly, 5 to 7 minutes or until thick and bubbly. Season gravy to taste. Serve gravy with Cornbread Dressing and turkey. Serves 12 to 14.

good gravy

Nobody likes lumpy gravy! If the gravy has lumps, pour it through a mesh tea strainer just before serving time.

Cranberry-Orange Glazed Cornish Hens

2 Cornish game hens
   (about 1¼ lbs. each)
2 T. butter or margarine, melted
1 t. salt
½ t. pepper
¼ c. whole-berry cranberry
   sauce

2 T. orange marmalade
1 T. lemon juice
1 t. dried, minced onion
1 t. cornstarch
11-oz. can mandarin oranges,
   drained

Remove and discard giblets and neck from hens; rinse hens with cold water and pat dry. Coat inside and outside of hens with butter; sprinkle outside with salt and pepper. Place hens, breast side down, on an ungreased rack in a shallow roasting pan. Insert a meat thermometer into meatiest portion of thigh of one hen; cover loosely with aluminum foil.

Bake at 375 degrees for 30 minutes; uncover and bake one more hour or until meat thermometer registers 180 degrees.

Meanwhile, combine cranberry sauce and next 4 ingredients in a small saucepan; bring to a boil. Reduce heat and simmer 2 minutes or until thickened and bubbly, stirring often. Stir in oranges. Spoon mixture over hens during last 20 minutes of baking. Serves 2 to 4.

garnish, if desired

Use simple garnishes to dress up main dishes throughout the year. Fresh mint sprigs add coolness and color to summertime dishes, while rosemary sprigs and cranberries arranged to resemble holly add a festive touch to holiday platters.

Cox's Memphis-in-May Ribs

When you serve ribs for company, make sure you have plenty of napkins and some moist towelettes for everyone. They're gonna be messy!

4 to 6 lbs. spareribs or back ribs	2 t. garlic powder
¼ c. paprika	2 t. white pepper
2 t. salt	2 t. black pepper
2 t. onion powder	1 t. cayenne pepper

Place ribs in a large shallow dish. Combine remaining ingredients in a small bowl; stir well. Rub paprika mixture over entire surface of ribs. Cover and chill 3 hours.

Preheat one side of charcoal or gas grill to medium heat (300 to 350 degrees). Place ribs on cool side of grill. Grill, covered with grill lid, over medium coals (300 to 350 degrees) for 2 to 2½ hours, turning every 30 minutes. Brush ribs with Barbecue Sauce during last 30 minutes of grilling time. Serve with additional Barbecue Sauce. Serves 4 to 6.

Barbecue Sauce:

2 c. water	3 T. salt
2 c. white vinegar	3 T. sugar
2 c. catsup	3 T. chili powder
½ c. onion, chopped	3 T. pepper

Combine all ingredients in a large saucepan. Bring to a boil; reduce heat and simmer, uncovered, 1½ hours, stirring often. Makes 3 cups.

Apricot-Glazed Pork Tenderloin & Couscous

A 2-ingredient glaze paints this pork with rich color and tangy-sweet flavor.

1¼-lb. pork tenderloin
1 T. olive oil
¼ t. salt
¼ t. pepper
⅓ c. apricot preserves

2 T. honey mustard
10-oz. pkg. couscous
½ c. dried apricots, diced
⅓ c. sliced almonds, toasted

Brush pork with olive oil; season with salt and pepper. Place on an aluminum foil-lined broiler pan.

Broil 5½ inches from heat 8 minutes or until browned, turning once.

Combine apricot preserves and honey mustard; spread over pork. Continue to broil 10 more minutes, turning once, or until a meat thermometer inserted in center of meat registers 155 degrees. Cover pork with aluminum foil and let stand 5 minutes.

Meanwhile, prepare couscous according to package directions. Fluff couscous; stir in apricots and almonds. Slice pork and serve with couscous. Serves 4.

handwritten menus

These lend a personal touch to any table. Cut colored papers to fit the front of old-fashioned milk bottles or Mason jars. Write the details on them and wrap them around the jars with a pretty ribbon...fill jars with water and flowers and arrange in the center of the table.

Fruited Pork Loin

½ c. dried dates, coarsely
    chopped
¼ c. dried apricots, coarsely
    chopped
¼ c. pecans, finely chopped
1 clove garlic, minced
1½ t. dried thyme, crushed

2 T. molasses, divided
½ t. salt, divided
¼ t. pepper
2-lb. boneless pork loin roast
⅔ c. bourbon or chicken broth
⅔ c. chicken broth
¼ c. whipping cream

Slices of this pork loin make a beautiful holiday presentation.

Tina

Blend together dates, apricots, pecans, garlic, thyme, one tablespoon molasses, ¼ teaspoon salt and pepper; set aside.

Butterfly pork loin roast by making a lengthwise cut down center of one side, cutting within ½ inch of the bottom. (Do not cut through roast.) Open roast, forming a rectangle. Starting at the center of the open loin, make another lengthwise cut on the left portion, cutting to within ½ inch of the edge. Repeat with right portion of the open loin. Spread date mixture evenly over open roast and starting with the short end, roll up stuffed roast jelly-roll style. Tie roast securely every 2 to 3 inches with kitchen string and place roast, seam side down, in a shallow roasting pan; set aside.

Blend together bourbon or chicken broth, ⅔ cup chicken broth and remaining one tablespoon molasses in a small saucepan. Bring mixture to a boil and pour over roast.

Roast pork at 350 degrees for one hour or until a meat thermometer inserted into thickest portion registers 150 degrees, basting occasionally. Remove roast from roasting pan; reserve drippings. Cover roast with aluminum foil and let stand 10 minutes or until thermometer registers 160 degrees before slicing.

Stir together cream and remaining ¼ teaspoon salt in a small saucepan; blend in reserved drippings. Cook over medium heat, stirring constantly, until mixture slightly thickens. Serve sauce with roast. Serves 6.

Tina Wright
Atlanta, GA

Pork Chops, Cabbage & Apples

3 t. paprika, divided
2 t. chopped fresh or 1 t. dried thyme, divided
2 t. kosher salt, divided
1½ t. pepper, divided
2 t. chopped fresh or 1 teaspoon dried sage, divided
6 (½-inch-thick) bone-in pork loin chops
2 slices bacon

1 head cabbage, coarsely chopped
2 onions, thinly sliced
1 Granny Smith apple, peeled and sliced
1 T. tomato paste
12-oz. bottle lager beer or 1½ c. apple cider
Optional: fresh thyme sprigs

Pork, cabbage and apples make a classic combination that's just delightful!

Jo Ann

Combine 2 teaspoons paprika, one teaspoon fresh or ½ teaspoon dried thyme, one teaspoon salt, one teaspoon pepper and one teaspoon fresh or ½ teaspoon dried sage; rub over pork chops.

Cook bacon slices in a large, deep skillet over medium-high heat 6 to 8 minutes or until crisp; remove bacon and drain on paper towels, reserving drippings in skillet. Crumble bacon.

Cook pork in hot drippings 3 minutes on each side or until browned and done; remove pork from skillet and keep warm.

Add cabbage, onions and apple to skillet. Cover and reduce heat to medium; cook, stirring occasionally, 15 minutes or until cabbage begins to wilt. Add tomato paste, beer or apple cider, bacon, remaining one teaspoon paprika, one teaspoon fresh or ½ teaspoon dried thyme, one teaspoon salt, ½ teaspoon pepper and one teaspoon fresh or ½ teaspoon dried sage, stirring to loosen particles from bottom of skillet. Cover and cook 15 minutes or until cabbage is tender and liquid is slightly thickened. Add pork and cook, uncovered, 5 minutes or until thoroughly heated. Garnish with fresh thyme sprigs, if desired. Serves 6.

Jo Ann
Gooseberry Patch

Mustard-Crusted Pork Roast & Browned Potatoes

4- to 5-lb. boneless pork loin
    roast
¾ t. salt, divided
¾ t. pepper, divided
½ c. coarse-grain mustard
8 cloves garlic, minced
3 T. olive oil

3 T. balsamic vinegar
3 T. fresh rosemary, chopped
    and divided
2 lbs. new potatoes
2 T. olive oil
Optional: fresh rosemary sprigs

Place pork in a greased roasting pan. Rub with ¼ teaspoon each salt and pepper. Combine mustard and next 4 ingredients in a small bowl; spread evenly over pork.

Peel a crosswise strip around each potato with a vegetable peeler, if desired. Cut each potato in half lengthwise. Toss potatoes with olive oil, one tablespoon chopped rosemary and ½ teaspoon each salt and pepper. Add to roasting pan around pork. Insert a meat thermometer into thickest part of roast.

Bake at 375 degrees for one hour to 1¼ hours or until thermometer registers 160 degrees. Let stand 10 minutes. Transfer roast to a serving platter. Surround pork with potatoes. Garnish with fresh rosemary sprigs, if desired. Serves 8 to 10.

eye-catching arrangements

It's easy to make oh-so-pretty floral arrangements by using unexpected containers. Instead of vases, try standing flowers in jars of water, then tuck the jars into simple shopping bags, formal top hats or vintage purses.

Festive Pork Roasts

(pictured on cover)

1½ c. dry red wine or beef broth
⅔ c. brown sugar, packed
½ c. water
½ c. catsup
¼ c. oil
4 cloves garlic, minced
3 T. soy sauce

2 t. curry powder
1 t. ground ginger
½ t. pepper
2 (2½- to 3-lb.) boneless rolled
    pork roasts
4 t. cornstarch
1½ c. water

Combine first 10 ingredients in a large shallow dish or plastic zipping bag; add pork. Cover or seal and chill 8 hours, turning occasionally.

Remove pork from marinade, reserving marinade to equal 2½ cups, adding water if necessary. Place pork on a rack in a shallow roasting pan lined with aluminum foil. Whisk reserved marinade into cornstarch in a small saucepan. Place pan over medium-high heat and bring sauce to a boil, whisking constantly. Cook, whisking constantly, 2 to 3 minutes or until thickened. Remove and reserve ¼ cup sauce. Set remaining sauce in saucepan aside.

Broil pork 6 inches from heat for 5 minutes. Pour water into bottom of pan. Reduce oven temperature to 325 degrees; bake 1¼ to 1½ hours or until a meat thermometer inserted into thickest portion registers 155 degrees, basting with reserved ¼ cup sauce during the last 15 minutes. Remove roast and let stand at least 10 minutes or until meat thermometer inserted into thickest portion registers 160 degrees. Serve with remaining warm sauce. Serves 8 to 10.

Ham with Bourbon, Cola & Cherry Glaze

12- to 14-lb. fully cooked, bone-
   in ham shank
1 T. black peppercorns
30 whole cloves
12-oz. can cola, divided
Optional: ¼ c. bourbon, divided

6 T. brown sugar, packed and
   divided
13-oz. jar cherry preserves,
   divided
Optional: kumquats, cherries

Remove skin from ham; trim fat to ¼"-thickness. Make shallow cuts in fat one inch apart in a diamond pattern. Place peppercorns in a small plastic zipping bag. Tap peppercorns with a meat mallet or small heavy skillet until coarsely crushed. Rub peppercorns over surface of ham; insert cloves in centers of diamonds. Insert a meat thermometer into ham, making sure it does not touch fat or bone. Place ham in a lightly greased 13"x9" pan; set aside.

Combine ¼ cup cola, 2 tablespoons bourbon, if using, and 2 table-spoons brown sugar; set aside. Combine remaining cola, bourbon, if using, and brown sugar; pour over ham. Bake at 350 degrees for 2 hours, basting with cola mixture every 15 minutes. Remove ham from oven; leave oven on. Meanwhile, combine reserved cola mixture and ⅔ cup cherry preserves in a medium saucepan. Cook over medium heat 3 minutes or until glaze is hot and sugar dissolves; brush ham with glaze. Return ham to oven; bake at 350 degrees for one hour and 45 more minutes or until thermometer registers 140 degrees. (Cover ham with aluminum foil during the last hour, if necessary, to prevent excessive browning.) Let ham stand one hour before carving.

Transfer baked ham to a serving platter; cover with foil. Remove fat from drippings in pan. Whisk remaining ½ cup cherry preserves into drippings in pan. Transfer mixture to a saucepan, if desired, or continue cooking in roasting pan placed over 2 burners on the stovetop. Bring to a boil; reduce heat and simmer until slightly thickened (8 to 10 minutes). Serve glaze with ham. Garnish with kumquats and cherries, if desired. Serves 12 to 14.

Vickie
Gooseberry Patch

This holiday ham sizzles with comfort! Pick a ham with a fat layer intact that will crisp up when baked and show off its pepper and clove crust.

Vickie

Mothers' Day

Spinach-Cheddar Quiche

Try using any of your favorite green, leafy vegetables for a unique taste!

2 c. shredded Cheddar cheese
2 T. all-purpose flour
10-oz. pkg. frozen chopped
    spinach, cooked and drained
1 c. milk
2 eggs, beaten

3 slices bacon, crisply cooked
    and crumbled
salt and pepper to taste
9-inch pie crust
Optional: paprika and chopped
    fresh parsley

In a large bowl, combine cheese and flour; add spinach, milk, eggs, bacon, salt and pepper. Blend well and pour into an unbaked pie crust. Bake at 350 degrees for one hour. Garnish with paprika and parsley, if desired. Serves 4.

Mary Rita Schlagel
Warwick, NY

Christmas

Cranberry Meatloaves

Individual
meatloaves for
each member
of the family!

Jodi

1 lb. ground beef
1 c. cooked rice
½ c. tomato juice
¼ c. onion, minced
1 egg

1 t. salt
16-oz. can whole-berry
    cranberry sauce
⅓ c. brown sugar, packed
1 T. lemon juice

Mix together ground beef, rice, tomato juice, onion, egg and salt. Shape mixture evenly into 5 mini meatloaves and place in a greased 13"x9" baking pan. Mix together cranberry sauce, brown sugar and lemon juice; spoon over top of each loaf. Bake at 350 degrees for 45 minutes. Serves 5.

Jodi Zarnoth-Hirsch
Chilton, WI

Baked Sausage & Eggs

6 breakfast sausage links
2 c. shredded sharp Cheddar
    cheese
1 T. all-purpose flour
1 c. shredded Monterey Jack
    cheese

6 eggs, lightly beaten
½ c. half-and-half
1 t. Worcestershire sauce

Cook sausage links according to package directions; drain on paper towels. Set sausage aside.

Combine Cheddar cheese and flour; sprinkle evenly in bottom of an ungreased shallow 1½-quart round casserole dish. Sprinkle with Monterey Jack cheese and set aside.

Combine eggs, half-and-half and Worcestershire sauce; pour over cheese mixture. Arrange sausages on top of egg mixture in spoke fashion. Cover and chill 8 hours.

Remove from refrigerator. Let stand, covered, at room temperature 30 minutes. Bake, uncovered, at 350 degrees for 45 minutes or until set and lightly golden. Let stand 5 minutes before serving. Serves 6.

Fathers' Day

Mexican Lasagna

1 lb. ground beef
16-oz. can refried beans
2 t. dried oregano
1 t. ground cumin
¾ t. garlic powder
2 c. picante sauce
1½ c. water

9 uncooked lasagna noodles
16-oz. container sour cream
¾ c. green onions, thinly sliced
2¼-oz. can sliced ripe olives,
  drained
1 c. shredded Monterey Jack
  cheese

Use a colorful
tablecloth or
runner and napkins
in vivid hues to
give the table a
Mexican flair.

Jo Ann

Cook ground beef in a large non-stick skillet, stirring until it
crumbles and is no longer pink; drain. Wipe skillet clean. Return beef
to skillet; stir in refried beans and seasonings.

Combine picante sauce and water. Pour 1⅓ cups picante mixture
into a lightly greased 13"x9" baking pan. Arrange 3 noodles over picante
mixture. Spread half of beef mixture evenly over noodles. Pour one
cup picante mixture over beef mixture and top with 3 more noodles.
Spread remaining beef mixture over noodles. Top with 3 remaining
noodles. Pour remaining 1⅓ cups picante mixture evenly over noodles.

Cover and bake at 350 degrees for 1½ hours.

Combine sour cream, green onions and ripe olives in a small bowl.
Remove lasagna from oven; spread sour cream mixture over lasagna
and sprinkle with cheese. Return to oven and bake 10 more minutes.
Let stand 10 minutes before serving. Serves 6.

Jo Ann
Gooseberry Patch

Tenderloin for Two with Peppercorn Cream

1 T. olive oil
2 (6-oz.) beef tenderloin steaks
salt and pepper to taste
¼ c. brandy or apple juice
1 clove garlic, minced
1 t. multi-colored peppercorns,
    crushed

½ t. dried oregano
⅛ t. salt
⅔ c. whipping cream
1½ T. sour cream
hot cooked rice
Optional: fresh oregano sprigs

Heat olive oil in a medium skillet until hot. Sprinkle tenderloin steaks with salt and pepper. Sear tenderloin steaks on both sides in skillet. Remove from skillet, reserving drippings in pan; place steaks on a rack in a broiler pan. Broil 5½ inches from heat 5 to 7 minutes on each side to desired degree of doneness.

Add brandy or apple juice to drippings in skillet; bring to a boil and use a spoon to loosen any remaining food on the bottom. Add minced garlic, peppercorns, oregano and salt; cook one minute. Add whipping cream; bring to a boil and cook 6 to 7 minutes or until sauce is reduced by half. Remove from heat. Whisk in sour cream and spoon sauce over steaks. Serve with rice. Garnish with fresh oregano sprigs, if desired. Serves 2.

Juicy Prime Rib

¼ c. cayenne pepper
2 T. salt
2 T. white pepper
1½ t. garlic powder

1½ t. dried thyme
1 t. onion powder
8- to 10-lb. boneless beef rib-eye
   roast

Combine first 6 ingredients; lightly press on top and sides of roast.

Place roast, fat side up, in a shallow roasting pan; insert a meat thermometer into the thickest part of roast, making sure it does not touch fat.

Bake, uncovered, at 425 degrees for 10 minutes. Reduce temperature to 325 degrees; bake 2 hours and 40 minutes or until thermometer registers 145 degrees (medium-rare) or 160 degrees (medium).

Remove roast to a serving platter. Let stand 15 minutes before carving. Serves 12 to 16.

Filet Mignon with Mushrooms

1 T. oil
8-oz. pkg. sliced mushrooms
4 cloves garlic, minced
4 (6-oz.) beef tenderloin filets

½ t. salt
½ t. pepper
½ t. garlic powder
⅓ c. Marsala wine or beef broth

Pour oil into a large skillet; place over medium-high heat until hot. Add mushrooms and garlic; cook 5 minutes or until liquid evaporates, stirring frequently. Remove from heat.

Meanwhile, sprinkle each filet with salt, pepper and garlic powder. Place filets on a lightly greased rack in a broiler pan; broil 3 inches from heat 5 to 6 minutes on each side or to desired degree of doneness.

Add wine or broth to mushroom mixture and bring to a boil; cook 2 minutes or until wine is almost absorbed. Place each filet on a serving plate and top with mushroom mixture. Serves 4.

Festive Cajun Pepper Steak

Cajun seasoning kicks up the flavor of saucy sirloin beef tips spooned over yummy mashed potatoes.

1½ lbs. sirloin beef tips
1 t. salt-free Cajun seasoning
1 T. oil
1 green pepper, chopped
1 onion, chopped
3 cloves garlic, minced
14½-oz. can diced tomatoes
14½-oz. can beef broth
2 t. Worcestershire sauce

1 t. white wine vinegar
½ t. dried basil
¼ t. salt
⅛ t. pepper
22-oz. pkg. refrigerated or frozen
    mashed potatoes
2 T. cornstarch
2 T. cold water

Sprinkle beef tips with Cajun seasoning. Cook beef in hot oil in a large skillet over medium-high heat 10 minutes or until browned. Add pepper, onion and garlic; sauté 3 minutes.

Stir in tomatoes with juice and next 6 ingredients. Bring to a boil; reduce heat, cover and simmer one hour or until meat is tender.

Prepare mashed potatoes according to package directions.

Stir together cornstarch and water until smooth; stir into meat mixture. Bring to a boil; cook, stirring constantly, 2 minutes or until thickened. Serve over mashed potatoes. Serves 4 to 6.

beyond the basics

Look past traditional napkins when hosting family & friends. Try using bandannas, colorful dish towels, inexpensive fabrics from the crafts store or, for especially saucy foods, moistened washcloths.

Chicken-Fried Steak

Authentic chicken-fried steak is crunchy outside, tender inside and served with plenty of cream gravy!

2¼ t. salt, divided	½ t. baking powder
1¾ t. pepper, divided	½ t. cayenne pepper
6 (4-oz.) cube steaks	4¾ c. milk, divided
1 sleeve saltine crackers, crushed	2 eggs
1¼ c. all-purpose flour, divided	3½ c. peanut oil

Sprinkle ¼ teaspoon each salt and black pepper over steaks. Set aside.

Combine cracker crumbs, one cup flour, baking powder, one teaspoon salt, ½ teaspoon black pepper and cayenne pepper.

Whisk together ¾ cup milk and eggs. Dredge steaks in cracker crumb mixture; dip in milk mixture and dredge in cracker mixture again.

Pour oil into a 12-inch skillet; heat to 360 degrees. (Do not use a non-stick skillet.) Fry steaks, in batches, 10 minutes. Turn and fry each batch 4 to 5 more minutes or until golden brown. Remove to a wire rack on a jelly-roll pan. Keep steaks warm in a 225-degree oven. Carefully drain hot oil, reserving cooked bits and one tablespoon drippings in skillet.

Whisk together remaining ¼ cup flour, one teaspoon salt, one teaspoon black pepper and 4 cups milk. Pour mixture into reserved drippings in skillet; cook over medium-high heat, whisking constantly, 10 to 12 minutes or until thickened. Serve gravy with steaks and mashed potatoes. Serves 6.

Black Beans 'n' Vegetable Chili, page 116

savory soups & sandwiches

Soups & sandwiches are great holiday food options, especially when you're serving a crowd. Make entertaining a little easier by hosting a casual Christmas party this year. Serve hearty bowls of 30-Minute Chili (page 131) with fresh-out-of-the-oven cornbread...the combination is sure to warm your guests right up! Celebrate Fathers' Day with a backyard picnic and enjoy scrumptious Grilled Cuban Sandwiches (page 143). They'll be a hit with Dad! Whatever the season or occasion, the recipes inside this chapter are just perfect for sharing with family & friends!

Black Beans 'n' Vegetable Chili
(pictured on page 114)

This vegetarian chili filled with black beans, bell peppers, squash and tomatoes and served over rice is hearty and filling.

1 onion, coarsely chopped
1 T. oil
28-oz. can diced tomatoes
⅔ c. picante sauce
1½ t. ground cumin
1 t. salt
½ t. dried basil
15-oz. can black beans, rinsed
    and drained
1 green pepper, cut into ¾-inch
    pieces

1 red pepper, cut into ¾-inch
    pieces
1 yellow squash or zucchini, cut
    into ½-inch pieces
hot cooked rice
Garnish: shredded Cheddar
    cheese, sour cream, chopped
    fresh cilantro
Optional: additional picante
    sauce

Sauté onion in oil in a Dutch oven over medium-high heat, stirring constantly, until tender. Add tomatoes with juice and next 4 ingredients; stir well. Bring to a boil; cover, reduce heat and simmer 5 minutes.

Stir in beans, peppers and squash. Cover and cook over medium-low heat 25 minutes or until vegetables are tender, stirring mixture occasionally.

To serve, ladle chili over rice in individual bowls. Top each serving with cheese, sour cream and cilantro. Serve with additional picante sauce, if desired. Makes 6 cups.

perfect pairings

Nothing goes better with hearty chili than warm cornbread! If you like your cornbread crisp, prepare it in a vintage sectioned cast-iron skillet…each wedge of cornbread will bake up with its own golden crust.

Easy Slow Cooker Potato Soup

4 to 5 potatoes, peeled and cubed
10¾-oz. can cream of celery soup
10¾-oz. can cream of chicken
   soup
1⅓ c. water

4⅔ c. milk
6.6-oz. pkg. instant mashed
   potato flakes
Optional: bacon bits, green onions,
   shredded Cheddar cheese

Place potatoes, soups and water in a 5-quart slow cooker. Cover and cook on high setting 2 to 3 hours or until potatoes are tender. Add milk and instant mashed potato flakes to reach desired consistency, stirring constantly. Cover and cook 2 to 3 hours longer; spoon into bowls to serve. Top with bacon bits, green onions and Cheddar cheese, if desired. Serves 4 to 6.

Tomato-Basil Soup

1½ c. sweet onions, diced
10 fresh basil leaves, chopped
3 cloves garlic, minced
28-oz. can whole tomatoes
2 (28-oz.) cans diced tomatoes
2 T. sugar

½ t. salt
½ t. pepper
¼ t. red pepper flakes
2 c. heavy whipping cream
Optional: garlic croutons or fresh
   basil leaves

Sauté onion, basil and garlic in a Dutch oven coated with non-stick vegetable spray about 8 minutes or until onion is tender. Process whole tomatoes with juice in a blender or food processor 10 seconds or until smooth. Add tomato purée, diced tomatoes with juice and sugar to onion mixture; simmer, uncovered, over low heat 2 hours. Add salt, pepper, red pepper flakes and heavy cream; cook until thoroughly heated. Garnish each serving with garlic croutons or fresh basil leaves, if desired. Makes 11 cups.

Whole Acorn Squash Cream Soup

*This unique recipe celebrates the beauty of squash by using it as a serving
bowl. Choose squash that stand upright for ease in baking and serving.*

4 acorn squash	1 c. chicken broth
¼ c. cream cheese	½ t. salt
1 c. heavy whipping cream	1 t. ground cinnamon

Cut off about one inch of stem ends of squash to reveal seeds.
Scoop out and discard seeds and pulp. Arrange squash in a
13"x9" baking pan.

Place one tablespoon cream cheese in each squash. Pour ¼ cup
each heavy cream and chicken broth over cream cheese in each
squash; sprinkle each with ⅛ teaspoon salt and ¼ teaspoon cinnamon.
Add water to baking pan to a depth of ½ inch.

Bake, uncovered, at 350 degrees for one hour and 45 minutes or
until squash are very tender.

To serve, carefully set each squash in a shallow soup bowl. Serves 4.

Butternut Squash Soup

A creamy, flavorful soup that is perfect to start a holiday meal.

Vickie

3-lb. butternut squash
8 carrots, peeled and cut into
    pieces
2½ c. chicken broth
¾ c. orange juice

½ t. salt
½ t. ground ginger
½ c. whipping cream
Optional: 2 T. finely chopped
    toasted pecans and nutmeg

Cut squash in half lengthwise; remove seeds. Place squash, cut sides down, in a shallow pan; add hot water to pan to a depth of ¾ inch. Cover with aluminum foil and bake at 400 degrees for 40 minutes or until tender; drain. Scoop out pulp; mash. Discard shell.

Cook carrots in boiling water 25 minutes or until tender; drain and mash.

Combine squash, carrots, chicken broth and next 3 ingredients in a bowl. Process half of mixture in a food processor or blender until smooth. Repeat procedure with remaining half of squash mixture.

Place puréed mixture in a large saucepan; bring to a simmer. Stir in cream; return to a simmer. Remove from heat.

To serve, ladle into individual bowls. Garnish with pecans and nutmeg, if desired. Makes 8 cups.

Vickie
Gooseberry Patch

seasonal menus

Thinking of a menu for guests? Let the season be your guide! Soups and stews brimming with the harvest's bounty are just right for fall get-togethers, and juicy fruit salads are delightful in the summer. Not only will you get the freshest ingredients when you plan by the season, but you'll also get the best prices at the supermarket!

Christmas Luncheon Crabmeat Bisque

6 T. butter, divided
1½ c. sliced mushrooms
¼ c. green pepper, finely
    chopped
¼ c. onion, finely chopped
1 green onion, chopped
2 T. fresh parsley, chopped
2 T. all-purpose flour

1 c. milk
1 t. salt
⅛ t. white pepper
⅛ t. hot pepper sauce
1½ c. half-and-half
1½ c. cooked crabmeat
Optional: 3 T. dry sherry

Heat 4 tablespoons butter in a large skillet. Add mushrooms, green pepper, onion, green onion and parsley; sauté 5 minutes or until vegetables are tender.

Heat remaining 2 tablespoons butter in a saucepan; stir in flour. Add milk and cook, stirring until thickened and smooth. Stir in salt, pepper and hot pepper sauce. Add sautéed vegetables and half-and-half. Bring to a boil, stirring constantly. Reduce heat to low; add crabmeat and simmer, uncovered, 5 minutes. Stir in sherry, if using, just before serving. Serves 4.

Seafood Gumbo

This recipe serves a party crowd. It freezes well if you happen to have leftovers.

1 gal. water	4 cloves garlic, minced
2 lemons, sliced	1 lb. cooked ham, cubed
3-oz. pkg. crab boil	2 lbs. fresh crabmeat, drained and flaked
3 t. salt, divided	
2 lbs. unpeeled shrimp, uncooked	3 lbs. okra, sliced
	28-oz. can whole tomatoes, undrained and chopped
1 lb. bacon	
1 c. all-purpose flour	½ c. Worcestershire sauce
2 onions, finely chopped	1 t. pepper
2 green peppers, finely chopped	hot cooked rice

Bring water, lemons, crab boil and one teaspoon salt to a boil in a large Dutch oven. Add shrimp and cook 3 to 5 minutes or until shrimp turn pink. Discard lemons and crab boil. Remove shrimp, reserving water. Peel shrimp. Chill.

Cook bacon in a large skillet until crisp; remove bacon, reserving drippings in skillet. Crumble bacon and set aside.

Add flour to drippings in skillet; cook over medium heat, stirring constantly, until caramel-colored (about 5 minutes). Stir in onion, pepper and garlic; cook over low heat 10 minutes or until vegetables are tender.

Add flour mixture and 2 teaspoons salt to reserved water in Dutch oven. Stir in remaining ingredients. Bring to a boil; reduce heat and simmer one hour and 50 minutes. Stir in chilled shrimp and cook 5 to 10 minutes. Serve gumbo over rice. Sprinkle with bacon. Makes 7½ quarts.

Passover

Matzo Ball Soup

3 stalks celery, sliced
2 carrots, peeled and sliced
2 parsnips, peeled and sliced
2 (32-oz.) jars kosher chicken
    broth
6 cloves garlic, minced
1 onion, chopped

¼ t. pepper
Optional: 3 c. cooked kosher
    chicken breast, shredded
4 fresh parsley sprigs
2 fresh thyme sprigs
1 fresh dill sprig
1 bay leaf

Combine first 7 ingredients and, if desired, chicken, in a large Dutch oven. Tie together parsley and next 3 ingredients with a string and place in Dutch oven. Bring mixture to a boil over medium-high heat; cover, reduce heat and simmer 30 minutes. Remove herbs and discard. Ladle soup into bowls and add 2 matzo balls per serving. Serves 7.

Matzo Balls:

4 eggs
½ c. seltzer water or water
½ c. butter, melted
1 t. salt
½ t. pepper

1 c. unsalted matzo meal
8 c. water
32-oz. container kosher chicken
    broth

Beat eggs with an electric mixer 2 minutes or until frothy. Add seltzer water and next 3 ingredients; beat well. Add matzo meal and beat until batter starts to thicken (about 2 minutes). Cover with plastic wrap and chill at least one hour.

Bring water and chicken broth to a boil in a large Dutch oven over medium-high heat. Reduce heat and simmer. Wet hands and shape batter into 14 (2-inch) balls. Drop balls into simmering broth mixture. Cover and cook 20 minutes or until matzo balls double in size. Add matzo balls to soup and discard cooking broth mixture. Makes 14 matzo balls.

Chicken & Wild Rice Soup

This slow-cooker soup makes filling holiday fare and is a good use for leftover turkey, too.

2 T. butter
3 stalks celery, thinly sliced
1 onion, chopped
8-oz. pkg. sliced fresh baby
    portobello mushrooms
2 t. garlic, minced
4 (14-oz.) cans seasoned chicken
    broth with roasted garlic
3 c. cooked chicken or turkey,
    chopped

1½ c. frozen corn, thawed and
    drained
8-oz. can sliced water chestnuts,
    drained
1 c. uncooked wild rice
1 t. salt
¾ t. pepper
2 c. whipping cream
Optional: toasted slivered
    almonds

Melt butter in a large skillet over medium-high heat. Add celery and onion; cook 4 minutes or until almost tender. Add mushrooms and garlic; cook 2 minutes.

Combine mushroom mixture, broth and next 6 ingredients in a 5-quart slow cooker.

Cover and cook on low setting 5 to 6 hours or until rice is tender. Stir in whipping cream. Garnish with toasted slivered almonds, if desired. Makes 12½ cups.

serving suggestion

When serving soups and stews, stack 2 or 3 cake stands, then fill each tier with a different type of roll for guests to try.

Chicken Tortilla Soup

1 c. red onion, chopped
1 red pepper, chopped
2 cloves garlic, minced
2 boneless, skinless chicken
    breasts
1 T. oil
7 c. chicken broth

9-oz. pkg. frozen corn, thawed
1 t. ground cumin
2 c. tortilla chips, lightly crushed
1 c. shredded Cheddar cheese
Optional: sour cream, chopped
    fresh cilantro

Sauté onion, pepper, garlic and chicken in oil in a Dutch oven
7 to 8 minutes; remove chicken. Pour in broth; bring to a simmer. Add
corn and cumin; cook 10 minutes. Shred chicken; stir into soup. Place
some chips in each bowl; ladle soup over chips. Sprinkle with cheese;
stir. Garnish with dollops of sour cream and sprinkle with cilantro,
if desired. Serves 6 to 8.

Lynnette Zeigler
South Lake Tahoe, CA

optional toppings

It's the unexpected touches that make the biggest impression. When serving
soup or chili, offer guests a variety of fun toppings...fill bowls with shredded
cheese, oyster crackers, chopped onions, sour cream and crunchy croutons.
Then invite everyone to dig in!

Turkey-Vegetable Chowder

This is a terrific, hearty chowder made using your leftover turkey!

Robyn

¼ c. butter
2 onions, chopped
2 T. all-purpose flour
1 t. curry powder
3 c. chicken broth
1 potato, chopped
1 c. carrots, thinly sliced
1 c. celery, thinly sliced

2 T. fresh parsley, minced
½ t. dried sage or poultry
  seasoning
3 c. cooked turkey, chopped
1½ c. half-and-half
10-oz. pkg. frozen chopped
  spinach
Optional: fresh parsley leaves

Melt butter in a small Dutch oven. Add onion and sauté 10 minutes. Stir in flour and curry powder. Cook 2 minutes. Add broth, potato, carrots, celery, parsley and sage. Reduce heat to low. Cover and simmer 10 to 15 minutes. Add turkey, half-and-half and frozen spinach. Cover and simmer, stirring occasionally, 10 minutes or until heated through. Garnish with fresh parsley leaves, if desired. Makes 8 cups.

Robyn Fiedler
Tacoma, WA

Halloween

Chow-Down Corn Chowder

6 slices bacon, diced
½ c. onion, chopped
2 c. potatoes, peeled and diced
2 10-oz. pkgs. frozen corn
16-oz. can cream-style corn

1¼ T. sugar
1½ t. Worcestershire sauce
1¼ t. seasoned salt
½ t. pepper
1 c. water

In a skillet, fry bacon until crisp. Remove bacon; reserve drippings. Add onion and potatoes to drippings and sauté about 5 minutes; drain well. Combine all ingredients in a 3½-quart slow cooker; stir well. Cover and cook on low setting 4 to 7 hours. Serves 4.

Marian Buckley
Fontana, CA

So easy to prepare with a slow cooker! It's delicious!

Marian

New Year's

Easy Brunswick Stew

Make preparation a breeze by stopping at your local supermarket deli or favorite barbecue restaurant for shredded pork.

3 lbs. shredded cooked pork
4 c. water
4 c. frozen diced potatoes
3 (14½-oz.) cans diced tomatoes
    with garlic and onion
14½-oz. can corn, drained

14½-oz. can cream-style corn
2 c. frozen lima beans
½ c. barbecue sauce
1 T. hot pepper sauce
1½ t. salt
1 t. pepper

Stir together all ingredients in a 6-quart stockpot. Bring stew to a boil; cover, reduce heat and simmer, stirring often, 45 minutes. Makes 5 quarts.

30-Minute Chili

A homemade seasoning mix gives this quick chili great taste.

2 lbs. lean ground beef
16-oz. can black beans
15½-oz. can small red beans
2 (14.5-oz.) cans diced tomatoes
    with green pepper, celery
    and onion

2 (8-oz.) cans tomato sauce
Optional: corn chips, shredded
    Cheddar cheese

Cook beef in a Dutch oven over medium-high heat, stirring often, 4 to 5 minutes or until beef crumbles and is no longer pink; drain well. Return beef to Dutch oven; sprinkle with ⅓ cup Chili Seasoning Mix. Cook one minute over medium-high heat.

Stir in undrained beans and remaining ingredients; bring to a boil over medium-high heat, stirring occasionally. Cover, reduce heat to low and simmer, stirring occasionally, 15 minutes. Top with corn chips and shredded Cheddar cheese, if desired. Serves 8.

Chili Seasoning Mix:

¾ c. chili powder
2 T. ground cumin
2 T. dried oregano
2 T. dried, minced onion

2 T. seasoned salt
2 T. sugar
2 T. dried, minced garlic

Stir undrained beans and remaining ingredients. Store seasoning mix in an airtight container up to 4 months at room temperature. Shake or stir well before using. Makes about 1⅓ cups.

Jo Ann
Gooseberry Patch

This versatile mix pairs perfectly with beef, pork, poultry or seafood!

Jo Ann

Eyeball Soup in a Slow Cooker

Don't be scared
away by this tasty
soup's name...the
eyeballs are
actually meatballs!

Sherry

2 lbs. lean ground beef
1 c. Italian-seasoned dry bread
    crumbs
1 egg, beaten
Optional: ¼ c. olive oil
3 stalks celery, sliced
1 green pepper, diced
1 c. carrots, peeled and diced
15¼-oz. can corn, drained
2 (14-oz.) cans beef broth
10-oz. can diced tomatoes with
    green chiles

4-oz. can diced green chiles
3 c. cooked rice
2 T. fresh cilantro, finely
    chopped
2 T. onion, minced
1 t. garlic powder
1 t. ground cumin
1 t. chili powder
1 t. salt
½ t. pepper
4 to 5 c. water

Combine ground beef, bread crumbs and egg; form into one-inch balls. Brown in a skillet over medium heat, adding oil, if desired; drain. Place meatballs in a 5-quart slow cooker and set aside. In a small saucepan, cover celery, green pepper and carrots with a little water. Cook until tender; add to slow cooker with remaining ingredients. Cover and cook on low setting 3 to 4 hours. Serves 8.

Sherry Sheehan
Phoenix, AZ

trick-or-treat tradition

Start a delicious soup supper tradition on Halloween night. Soup stays simmering hot while you hand out treats, and it isn't too filling...everyone has room to nibble on goodies!

Cucumber Sandwiches

Cold cucumber sandwiches are one of the ultimate feel-good foods that strike a chord with ladies of all ages.

1 cucumber, peeled, seeded and
    grated
8-oz. pkg. cream cheese,
    softened
1 T. mayonnaise

1 small shallot, minced
¼ t. seasoned salt
16-oz. loaf sandwich bread
Optional: cucumber slices

    Drain cucumber well, pressing between layers of paper towels.

    Stir together cucumber and next 4 ingredients. Spread mixture over half of bread slices. Top with remaining bread slices.

    Trim crusts from sandwiches; cut sandwiches in half diagonally. Garnish with cucumber slices, if desired. Store sandwiches in an airtight container in refrigerator. Serves 16.

Mark's Egg Salad Sandwiches

6 eggs, hard-boiled, peeled and chopped
⅓ c. celery, finely chopped
⅓ c. onion, finely chopped
3 to 4 T. mayonnaise-type salad dressing
1 to 2 t. mustard

1 t. Worcestershire sauce
½ t. salt
¼ t. pepper
½ t. dry mustard
1 T. dill weed
1 loaf sliced bread

I must confess...this is my husband's recipe. It's so delicious!

Connie

Mix all ingredients except bread in a small bowl; refrigerate about one hour. Spread on bread. Serves 6 to 8.

Connie Herek
Bay City, MI

sandwich smorgasbord

Whip up several different kinds of sandwiches (or stop at the local deli for a few!) and cut each one into 4 sections. Arrange them all on a large platter with chips and pickles...everyone will love the variety, and the preparation couldn't be easier.

Creamy Tuna Melts

2 to 3 stalks celery, diced
1 onion, diced
12-oz. can tuna, drained
½ c. cottage cheese
½ c. mayonnaise

¼ t. garlic salt
⅛ t. sugar
4 English muffins, split and
   toasted
8 slices American cheese

In a skillet sprayed with non-stick vegetable spray, sauté celery and onion until tender. Add tuna, cottage cheese, mayonnaise, garlic salt and sugar to skillet. Mix well, breaking up tuna. Cook over low heat until warmed through, stirring frequently; remove from heat. Place toasted muffins cut sides up on a broiler pan. Spread with tuna mixture; top with cheese slices. Broil until cheese melts; serve immediately. Serves 8.

Cindy Atkins
Vancouver, WA

Fancy Chicken Salad

Delicious as either a sandwich filling or a salad.

Andrea

2 c. cooked chicken, diced
½ c. celery, diced
⅓ c. seedless grapes, halved
2 green onions, sliced
⅓ c. slivered almonds

½ c. mayonnaise
½ t. Worcestershire sauce
½ t. curry powder
salt and pepper to taste

Combine chicken, celery, grapes, onions and almonds. Blend in mayonnaise, Worcestershire sauce and curry powder; add salt and pepper to taste. Serves 4 to 6.

Andrea Miller
Sugar Land, TX

Mothers' Day

Turkey-Veggie Bagels

Instead of bagels, you can also slice a loaf of round bread in half and layer on all the goodies. Replace the top of the loaf, cut into wedges and secure the sandwich in plastic wrap...an easy take-along lunch.

4 onion bagels, sliced in half
4 leaves romaine lettuce
8 slices smoked deli turkey
1 cucumber, thinly sliced

2 to 4 radishes, thinly sliced
1 to 2 carrots, shredded
¼ c. cream cheese with chives
   and onions

Arrange 4 bagel halves on a serving tray. Place a lettuce leaf on each; top with turkey, cucumber, radish and carrot. Spread cream cheese on top halves of bagels; place on bottom halves. Serves 4.

April Jacobs
Loveland, CO

quick solutions

Easiest-ever sandwiches for a get-together...provide a big platter of cold cuts, a basket of fresh breads and a choice of condiments so guests can make their own. Add cups of hot soup plus cookies for dessert...done!

Thanksgiving

Turkey Panini

Use leftover turkey after a big holiday feast for these delicious sandwiches. Pile on the turkey and use your homemade cranberry sauce, if desired. Shaved deli turkey is a fine substitute.

¼ c. whole-berry cranberry
    sauce
2 to 3 t. horseradish
2 T. mayonnaise
4 (½-inch-thick) large slices
    ciabatta bread
4 (⅜-inch-thick) slices cooked
    turkey breast or deli turkey

salt and pepper to taste
4 slices provolone cheese
4 slices bacon, cooked
1½ T. olive oil
Optional: mixed salad greens

Preheat panini press according to manufacturer's instructions. Combine cranberry sauce and horseradish, stirring well.

Spread mayonnaise on one side of each slice of bread. Spread cranberry-horseradish sauce on 2 slices of bread; top each sandwich with 2 turkey slices and sprinkle with salt and pepper.

Arrange 2 cheese slices on each sandwich; top with 2 bacon slices. Cover with tops of bread, mayonnaise side down.

Brush tops of sandwiches with olive oil. Turn and brush bottoms of sandwiches with olive oil.

Place sandwiches in panini press; cook 3 minutes or until cheese begins to melt and bread is toasted. Serve hot. Garnish with mixed salad greens, if desired. Makes 2 sandwiches.

Tailgate Party Sandwiches

Easy to make and everyone always wants the recipe!

Laurie

1 onion, chopped
½ c. butter, softened
2 T. poppy seed
1 T. mustard

1 T. Worcestershire sauce
20 to 24 dinner rolls, halved
1 lb. baked ham, shaved
8-oz. pkg. sliced Swiss cheese

Combine onion, butter, poppy seed, mustard and Worcestershire sauce; spread mixture on both sides of rolls. Cover one side with ham; place cheese over top. Replace tops of rolls; arrange on ungreased baking sheets. Bake at 400 degrees for 25 to 30 minutes or until cheese is melted; separate rolls before serving. Makes 20 to 24 sandwiches.

Laurie Michael
Colorado Springs, CO

Toasty Ham & Swiss Stacks

2 T. mayonnaise
4 t. Dijon mustard
2 t. fresh dill, finely chopped
salt and pepper to taste
1 lb. sliced mushrooms

2 T. olive oil
8 slices rye bread, toasted
4 slices deli ham
4 slices Swiss cheese
4 thin slices red onion

In a small bowl, whisk together mayonnaise, mustard, dill, salt and pepper; set aside. In a skillet over medium-high heat, sauté mushrooms in oil, stirring occasionally, 5 minutes or until liquid evaporates; remove from heat. Spread 4 toast slices with mayonnaise mixture. Layer each slice with ham, mushrooms, cheese and onion. Place on an ungreased baking sheet. Broil under a preheated broiler, about 4 inches from heat, one to 2 minutes or until golden and cheese is melted. Top with remaining toast slices. Serves 4.

Scrumptious Sandwich Loaves

You'll feed quite a crowd with these sandwiches...easy to make ahead, too!

2 loaves Italian bread
8-oz. pkg. cream cheese,
    softened
1 c. shredded Cheddar cheese
¾ c. green onions, chopped

¼ c. mayonnaise
1 T. Worcestershire sauce
1 lb. sliced deli ham
1 lb. sliced roast beef
¼ to ½ c. sliced dill pickles

Cut loaves in half lengthwise; hollow out halves. Set aside. Combine cheeses, onions, mayonnaise and Worcestershire sauce; spread over both halves of bread. Layer ham, beef and pickles on bottom halves of bread; press on top halves. Wrap in plastic wrap; refrigerate at least 2 hours. Cut into 1½- to 2-inch slices. Serves 12 to 14.

Dee Ann Ice
Delaware, OH

for the family on-the-run

If family members will be dining at different times, fix sandwiches ahead of time, wrap in aluminum foil and refrigerate. Pop them into a toaster oven or under a broiler to heat...fresh, tasty and ready when you are!

Grilled Cuban Sandwiches

A great combination of flavors…some Cuban sandwiches have layers of thinly sliced cooked pork, too. You can also grill sandwiches on a countertop grill or a panini press.

1 loaf French bread, halved
    lengthwise
2 T. Dijon mustard

6 oz. Swiss cheese, thinly sliced
6 oz. deli ham, sliced
8 dill pickle sandwich slices

Spread cut sides of bread with mustard. Arrange half each of cheese and ham on bottom half of bread; top with pickle slices. Repeat layering with remaining cheese and ham; cover with top half of bread. Slice into quarters. Arrange sandwiches in a skillet that has been sprayed with non-stick vegetable spray; place a heavy skillet on top of sandwiches. Cook over medium-high heat 2 minutes on each side, or until golden and cheese is melted. Serves 4.

Gladys Kielar
Perrysburg, OH

delicious dip

A fast-fix veggie dip that's yummy! Stir together 1¼ cups sour cream with ½ cup mayonnaise and a one-ounce package of dry onion soup mix. Spoon dip into a serving bowl and garnish with minced chives.

Easy Southern-Style Pork Barbecue

This Southern slow-cooker favorite is known as pulled pork barbecue.

3- to 4-lb. pork roast
¼ c. water
2 T. smoke-flavored cooking sauce
pepper to taste
6 to 8 hamburger buns, split
Optional: favorite barbecue sauce, coleslaw

Place pork roast in a 4- to 5-quart slow cooker. Add water; sprinkle evenly with cooking sauce and pepper to taste. Cover and cook on high one hour, then on low 6 to 8 hours. Remove roast from slow cooker; shred meat and pull from the bone with a fork. Place meat on hamburger buns; top with barbecue sauce and a scoop of coleslaw, if desired. Serves 6 to 8.

Marilyn Morel
Keene, NH

Delicious BBQ Hamburgers

1 lb. ground beef
½ c. milk
½ c. bread crumbs
¼ t. pepper
¼ t. garlic powder
½ c. onion, chopped
½ c. green pepper, chopped
1 c. catsup
2 t. vinegar
2 t. mustard
½ c. sugar
¾ t. salt

Combine beef, milk, bread crumbs, pepper, garlic powder, onion and green pepper; mix well. Shape into patties and place in a skillet; brown both sides. Place in a greased 13"x9" baking pan; set aside. Combine catsup and remaining ingredients in a mixing bowl; pour over patties. Bake at 350 degrees for one hour. Serves 4 to 6.

Dee Ann Ice
Delaware, OH

Slow Cooker Sloppy Joes

3 c. celery, chopped
1 c. onion, chopped
1 c. catsup
1 c. barbecue sauce
1 c. water
2 T. vinegar
2 T. Worcestershire sauce
2 T. brown sugar, packed
1 t. chili powder
1 t. salt
1 t. pepper
½ t. garlic powder
3- to 4-lb. boneless chuck roast
14 to 18 hamburger buns
Garnishes: banana peppers, sliced
    olives, carrot crinkles, pretzel
    sticks, sliced pimentos, fresh
    parsley sprigs

Combine the first 12 ingredients in a 4- to 5-quart slow cooker; mix well. Add roast; cover and cook on high setting 6 to 7 hours or until tender. Remove roast; shred meat, return to slow cooker and heat through. Serve on hamburger buns. Garnish, if desired. Serves 14 to 18.

Lynda Robson
Boston, MA

Layered Cornbread &
Turkey Salad, page 180

splendid sides & salads

Round out your holiday meals with any of the tasty sides & salads in this chapter.

Sweet & savory options like Glazed Carrots (page 153) and Crumb-Topped

Spinach Casserole (page 165) make wonderful additions to the Christmas Day

sideboard. Fresh Corn Salad (page 185) is the perfect

summertime dish to complement all your favorite

grilled meats. Use leftover turkey from Thanksgiving

dinner to make Layered Cornbread &

Turkey Salad (page 180). Flip through

this chapter to find old & new favorites

to prepare throughout the year.

Dad's Braggin' Beans

½ lb. hot ground pork sausage
1 Vidalia or other sweet onion,
    chopped
2 (16-oz.) cans pork and beans
15-oz. can black beans, drained
½ c. dark brown sugar, packed
½ c. hickory-smoked barbecue
    sauce

⅓ c. catsup
¼ c. coarse-grain mustard
¼ c. molasses
1 jalapeño pepper, minced
1 to 2 t. chili powder
4 slices bacon

Brown sausage and onion in a skillet, stirring until sausage crumbles. Drain. Combine sausage mixture, undrained pork and beans and next 8 ingredients in an ungreased 2½-quart casserole dish; stir well. Place bacon across top of beans. Bake, uncovered, at 350 degrees for 2 hours or until desired thickness. Serves 6.

Butter Beans with Cornbread Crust

For a fresh option, look for speckled butter beans late in the summer at your local farmers' market. Simmer the fresh beans a few minutes less.

4 c. chicken broth
2 (16-oz.) pkgs. frozen butter
   beans
½ t. salt

½ t. pepper
1 sweet onion, diced
1 poblano chile, diced
1 T. olive oil

Bring first 4 ingredients to a boil in a large saucepan over medium-high heat. Reduce heat to low; cover and simmer 25 minutes or until beans are tender. Remove from heat.

Sauté onion and chile in hot oil in a large skillet over medium-high heat 2 minutes; remove from heat and stir into beans. Spoon bean mixture into a lightly greased 13"x9" baking pan.

Spoon Cornbread Crust Batter over beans, spreading to edges of pan. Bake, uncovered, at 425 degrees for 20 minutes or until crust is golden. Serves 6 to 8.

Cornbread Crust Batter:

2 c. cornbread mix
½ c. buttermilk

½ c. sour cream
2 eggs, lightly beaten

Stir together all ingredients. Makes 3 cups.

Easy Fancy Broccoli

⅓ c. pine nuts

¼ c. butter

1 T. olive oil

6 cloves garlic, thinly sliced

1 lb. broccoli flowerets

½ t. salt

⅛ t. red pepper flakes

Toast pine nuts in a large skillet over medium heat 6 minutes or until lightly browned. Remove from skillet and set aside.

Heat butter and oil in same skillet over medium heat until butter melts. Add garlic; sauté one to 2 minutes or until lightly browned. Add broccoli, salt and red pepper flakes. Sauté 8 minutes or until broccoli is tender. Stir in pine nuts before serving. Serves 6.

Jo Ann
Gooseberry Patch

Bagged broccoli flowerets make this side dish a cinch to prepare!

Jo Ann

eat your veggies!

Get kids to eat their vegetables! Serve fresh cut-up vegetables with small cups of creamy salad dressing or even peanut butter for dipping.

Brussels Sprouts au Gratin

Brussels sprouts have never looked as good as they do smothered in this yummy cheese sauce and capped with crumbs. If you prefer, substitute regular Worcestershire sauce for the white wine variety

¼ c. dry bread crumbs

1 T. grated Parmesan cheese

2 lbs. fresh Brussels sprouts, trimmed and halved lengthwise

2 T. butter or margarine

2 T. all-purpose flour

1½ c. milk

1 c. shredded Gruyère or Swiss cheese

1 T. white wine Worcestershire sauce

½ t. salt

¼ t. pepper

¼ t. paprika

Combine bread crumbs and Parmesan cheese; set aside.

Cook Brussels sprouts in boiling water to cover 12 minutes or until barely tender. Drain and place in a lightly greased 1½-quart gratin dish or an 11"x7" baking pan. Set aside.

Melt butter in a saucepan over low heat; add flour, stirring until smooth. Cook, stirring constantly, one minute. Gradually add milk; cook over medium heat, stirring constantly, until thickened and bubbly.

Add Gruyère cheese and next 3 ingredients, stirring until cheese melts.

Spoon sauce over Brussels sprouts; sprinkle with bread crumb mixture and paprika. Bake, uncovered, at 350 degrees for 20 minutes or until golden and bubbly. Serves 8.

Note: Three 10-ounce packages of frozen Brussels sprouts can be substituted for fresh sprouts, if desired. Just prepare according to package directions before assembling the casserole.

Baked Butternut Squash & Apples

2 butternut squash, peeled
    and seeded
2¼ lbs. Granny Smith apples,
    peeled and cored
¾ c. dried currants

nutmeg to taste
salt and pepper to taste
¾ c. maple syrup
¼ c. butter, cut into pieces
1½ T. fresh lemon juice

This is an old-fashioned recipe from the Midwest; the apples and maple syrup are wonderful together!

Vickie

Cut squash and apples crosswise into ¼-inch-thick slices. Cook squash in a large pot of boiling, salted water 3 minutes or until almost tender. Drain well. Combine squash, apples and currants in a 13"x9" glass baking pan. Season with desired amounts of nutmeg, salt and pepper. Combine maple syrup, butter and lemon juice in a small saucepan. Whisk over low heat until butter melts. Pour syrup over squash mixture and toss to coat evenly. Bake, uncovered, at 350 degrees until squash and apples are very tender, about one hour, stirring occasionally. Cool 5 minutes. Serves 8.

Vickie
Gooseberry Patch

Glazed Carrots

1-lb. pkg. baby carrots
1 c. water
1 t. orange zest
¼ c. orange juice
2 t. butter

2 t. honey
1 to 3 t. fresh ginger, grated
¼ t. salt
⅛ t. pepper

Combine all ingredients in a medium saucepan; bring to a boil over medium-high heat. Reduce heat and simmer, stirring occasionally, 30 to 35 minutes or until liquid just evaporates and carrots are glazed. Serves 4.

Corn Pudding

If you have it, try this dish using fresh sweet corn. Yum!

9 ears corn

4 eggs, beaten

½ c. half-and-half

1½ t. baking powder

⅓ c. butter

2 T. sugar

2 T. all-purpose flour

1 T. butter, melted

⅛ t. pepper

Remove and discard husks and silks from corn. Cut off tips of corn kernels into a bowl; scrape milk and remaining pulp from cob with a paring knife to measure 3 to 4 cups total. Set corn aside.

Combine eggs, half-and-half and baking powder, stirring well with a wire whisk.

Melt ⅓ cup butter in a large saucepan over low heat; add sugar and flour, stirring until smooth. Remove from heat; gradually add egg mixture, whisking constantly until smooth. Stir in corn.

Pour corn mixture into a greased one- or 1½-quart casserole dish.

Bake, uncovered, at 350 degrees for 40 to 45 minutes or until pudding is set. Drizzle with melted butter; sprinkle with pepper.

Broil 5½ inches from heat 2 minutes or until golden. Let stand 5 minutes before serving. Serves 6 to 8.

Cornbread Dressing
(pictured on page 74)

This Southern classic is a Thanksgiving dinner favorite. This version is quite moist; if you prefer a firmer dressing, use only 4 cans of broth.

1 c. butter, divided
3 c. white cornmeal
1 c. all-purpose flour
2 T. sugar
2 t. baking powder
1½ t. salt
1 t. baking soda
7 eggs, divided
3 c. buttermilk

3 c. soft bread crumbs
3 c. celery, finely chopped
2 c. onion, finely chopped
½ c. fresh sage, finely chopped
   or 1 T. dried rubbed sage
5 (10½-oz.) cans condensed
   chicken broth, undiluted
1 T. pepper

Place ½ cup butter in a 13"x9" baking dish; heat in oven at 425 degrees for 4 minutes.

Combine cornmeal and next 5 ingredients; whisk in 3 eggs and buttermilk. Pour hot butter from pan into batter, stirring until blended. Pour batter into pan. Bake at 425 degrees for 30 minutes or until golden. Cool.

Crumble cornbread into a large bowl; stir in bread crumbs and set aside.

Melt remaining ½ cup butter in a large skillet over medium heat; add celery and onion and sauté until tender. Stir in sage and sauté one more minute.

Stir vegetables, remaining 4 eggs, chicken broth and pepper into cornbread mixture; spoon into one lightly greased 13"x9" baking pan and one lightly greased 8"x8" baking pan. Cover and chill 8 hours, if desired.

Bake dressing, uncovered, at 375 degrees for 35 to 40 minutes or until golden. Serves 16 to 18.

Green Bean-Corn Casserole

Try this quick & easy side dish.

14½-oz. can French-style green beans, drained
15¼-oz. can corn, drained
1 c. shredded sharp Cheddar cheese
½ c. onion, chopped
1 c. sour cream
8-oz. can sliced water chestnuts, drained
10¾-oz. can cream of celery soup
½ c. butter, melted
1 sleeve round buttery crackers, crushed

Spread green beans on the bottom of an ungreased 13"x9" baking pan; layer corn on top. In a bowl, combine cheese, onion, sour cream, water chestnuts and celery soup; spread over the vegetables. Combine butter and crackers; sprinkle on top. Bake at 400 degrees for 40 minutes or until golden. Serves 6.

Jennifer Thomas
Coffeyville, KS

A terrific change from the more traditional green bean casseroles.

Jennifer

veggie market

Take the kids along to a farmers' market. Let each choose a vegetable and help prepare it...even picky eaters will want to eat their very own prepared dish.

Homestyle Green Beans

This is a tasty way to serve fresh green beans.

2 lbs. green beans, trimmed
2 c. water
1¼ t. salt, divided
⅓ c. butter or margarine
1½ T. sugar

1 t. dried basil
½ t. garlic powder
¼ t. pepper
2 c. cherry or grape tomatoes, halved

Place beans in a Dutch oven; add water and one teaspoon salt. Bring to a boil; cover, reduce heat and simmer 15 minutes or until tender. Drain; keep warm.

Melt butter in a saucepan over medium heat; stir in sugar, basil, garlic powder, remaining ¼ teaspoon salt and pepper. Add tomatoes and cook, stirring gently until thoroughly heated.

Pour tomato mixture over beans and toss gently. Serve hot. Serves 8.

Black-Eyed Peas with Caramelized Onions & Country Ham

3 (15.8-oz.) cans black-eyed peas
1 bay leaf
14-oz. can chicken broth
2 T. olive oil
1 red onion, diced
¼ lb. country ham, diced

½ c. balsamic vinegar
1½ t. fresh thyme, chopped or
   ½ t. dried thyme
½ t. pepper
Optional: fresh thyme sprigs

Combine first 3 ingredients in a 2-quart saucepan; bring to a boil. Cover, reduce heat and simmer 10 minutes; drain. Discard bay leaf. Return peas to pan; cover and set aside.

Meanwhile, heat oil in a large skillet over medium-high heat. Add onion; cook 5 minutes or until golden, stirring often. Reduce heat; add ham and cook 10 more minutes or until ham is crisp and onion is well browned. Stir in vinegar, chopped thyme and pepper; bring to a boil. Cook 5 minutes or until liquid is a thin syrup, stirring occasionally to loosen any caramelized bits from bottom of pan. Pour over peas; toss well. Garnish with fresh thyme sprigs, if desired. Serves 8.

Garlic-Basil Mashed Potatoes

1 large bulb garlic, unpeeled
2 T. olive oil
9 redskin potatoes, peeled and
    chopped
1 t. salt, divided

8-oz. container sour cream
½ c. grated Parmesan cheese
½ c. milk
¼ c. fresh basil leaves, chopped

Cut off pointed end of garlic; place garlic on a piece of aluminum foil and drizzle with oil. Fold foil to seal. Bake at 350 degrees for 40 minutes; cool 10 minutes. Squeeze pulp from cloves garlic and mash with a fork.

Meanwhile, place potatoes and ½ teaspoon salt in a Dutch oven; cover potatoes with water and boil 25 minutes or until tender. Drain well. Return potatoes to pan. Mash potatoes; stir in roasted garlic, ½ teaspoon salt, sour cream and Parmesan cheese. Gradually stir in milk; add basil, stirring gently.

Spoon potato mixture into a lightly greased 13"x9" baking pan. Bake, uncovered, at 350 degrees for 25 minutes or until hot and bubbly. Serves 8 to 10.

Jo Ann
Gooseberry Patch

Mashed potatoes are a very popular comfort food at Gooseberry Patch potlucks; we're always looking for new ways to serve them! Try this recipe...we think you'll like the garlic and basil combination.

Jo Ann

Scalloped Potatoes with Ham

1 onion, chopped
1 T. oil
3 cloves garlic, finely chopped
2 sweet potatoes, peeled and cut
    into ¼-inch slices
2 potatoes, peeled and cut into
    ¼-inch slices
½ c. all-purpose flour

1 t. salt
¼ t. pepper
2 c. cooked ham, chopped
2 c. shredded Gruyère cheese,
    divided
1¾ c. whipping cream
2 T. butter, cut into pieces

Sauté onion in oil in a saucepan over medium-high heat 5 minutes or until tender. Add garlic; cook 30 seconds. Remove from heat and set aside. Place potatoes in a large bowl.

Combine flour, salt and pepper; sprinkle over potatoes, tossing to coat. Arrange half of potato mixture in a greased 13"x9" baking pan or 3-quart gratin dish. Top with onion, ham and one cup cheese. Top with remaining potato mixture. Pour cream over potato mixture. Dot with butter; cover with aluminum foil.

Bake at 400 degrees for 50 minutes. Uncover, top with remaining one cup cheese and bake 20 more minutes or until potatoes are tender and cheese is golden. Let stand 10 minutes before serving. Serves 6.

Au Gratin Potato Casserole

(pictured on cover)

32-oz. pkg. frozen diced
   potatoes
16-oz. container sour cream
2 c. shredded Cheddar cheese
10¾-oz. can cream of mushroom
   soup

1 onion, finely chopped
¼ t. freshly ground pepper
2 c. crushed corn flake cereal
¼ c. butter, melted

Stir together first 6 ingredients in a large bowl. Spoon potato mixture into a lightly greased 13"x9" baking pan. Sprinkle evenly with crushed corn flake cereal and drizzle evenly with butter.

Bake, uncovered, at 325 degrees for one hour and 20 minutes or until bubbly. Serves 10 to 12.

Perfect Potato Latkes

4 potatoes, peeled
1 onion
¼ c. biscuit baking mix
2 eggs, lightly beaten

peanut oil
Optional: applesauce, sour
   cream

Shred potatoes and onion in a food processor; drain well.

Stir together biscuit baking mix and egg; add potato and onion.

Pour peanut oil to a depth of ½ inch in a large, heavy skillet. Drop potato mixture by tablespoonfuls into hot oil; fry mixture, in batches, over medium heat 2 minutes on each side or until golden. Drain latkes on paper towels. Serve latkes with applesauce and sour cream, if desired. Serves 10 to 12.

Crumb-Topped Spinach Casserole

This quick, cheesy side, with its crunchy browned topping, can be ready to bake in just over the time it takes to preheat the oven.

2 T. butter
1 onion, chopped
2 cloves garlic, minced
8-oz. pkg. cream cheese, softened
2 T. all-purpose flour
2 eggs
½ t. salt
¼ t. pepper

1 c. milk
4 (10-oz.) pkgs. frozen chopped spinach, thawed and drained
8-oz. pkg. shredded Cheddar cheese
1 c. Italian-seasoned Japanese bread crumbs (panko) or dry bread crumbs
3 to 4 T. butter, melted

Melt 2 tablespoons butter in a large non-stick skillet over medium heat. Add onion and garlic; sauté 8 minutes or until tender.

Stir together cream cheese and flour in a large bowl until smooth. Whisk in eggs, salt and pepper. Gradually whisk in milk until blended. Add sautéed onion and garlic, spinach and Cheddar cheese, stirring until blended. Spoon into a lightly greased 11"x7" baking pan.

Combine bread crumbs and melted butter in a small bowl; toss well. Sprinkle over casserole.

Bake, uncovered, at 350 degrees for 30 to 35 minutes or until thoroughly heated and bread crumbs are golden. Serves 8 to 10.

Note: To make individual spinach casseroles, spoon spinach mixture into 8 (8-ounce) lightly greased ramekins; top each with buttered bread crumbs. Bake, uncovered, at 375 degrees for 25 to 30 minutes or until golden.

Jo Ann
Gooseberry Patch

This recipe is the one to introduce kids to spinach.

Jo Ann

Squash Casserole

There's something about a classic vegetable casserole that's impossible to resist.

1½ lbs. yellow squash, cut into
    ¼-inch slices
1 lb. zucchini, cut into ¼-inch
    slices
1 sweet onion, chopped
2½ t. salt, divided
1 c. carrots, grated
10¾-oz. can cream of chicken
    soup

8-oz. container sour cream
8-oz. can water chestnuts,
    drained and chopped
8-oz. pkg. herb-flavored
    stuffing mix
½ c. butter, melted

Even picky eaters go back for second helpings!

Vickie

Place squash and zucchini in a Dutch oven. Add chopped onion, 2 teaspoons salt and water to cover. Bring to a boil over medium-high heat and cook 5 minutes; drain well.

Stir together carrot, next 3 ingredients and remaining ½ teaspoon salt in a large bowl; fold in squash mixture. Stir together stuffing mix and melted butter; spoon half of stuffing mixture into bottom of a lightly greased 13"x9" baking pan. Spoon squash mixture over stuffing mixture and top with remaining stuffing mixture.

Bake at 350 degrees for 30 to 35 minutes or until bubbly and golden, covering with aluminum foil after 20 to 25 minutes to prevent excessive browning, if necessary. Let stand 10 minutes before serving. Serves 8.

Vickie
Gooseberry Patch

keep it hot

If you're taking a casserole to a potluck dinner or picnic, keep it toasty by covering the casserole dish with aluminum foil and then wrapping it in several layers of newspaper.

Roasted Vegetables

Easy to assemble and bake while you are finishing other items for dinner.

1½ lbs. sweet potatoes, peeled
    and cut into 1½-inch pieces
¾ lb. turnips, peeled and cut into
    1½-inch pieces
1 onion, peeled and cut into
    1½-inch wedges

6 cloves garlic
3 T. olive oil
1 T. fresh rosemary, chopped
1 T. fresh oregano or marjoram,
    chopped
1 t. salt

Combine first 5 ingredients in a large bowl; toss well. Place vegetables in a single layer in a large roasting pan or broiler pan. Bake at 450 degrees for 25 to 30 minutes or until vegetables are tender, stirring gently every 10 minutes. Stir in herbs and salt just before serving. Serves 6.

Creamy Southern Grits

2 c. half-and-half or whipping
    cream
¼ t. salt
⅛ t. garlic powder
⅛ t. pepper
½ c. quick-cooking grits,
    uncooked

2 oz. cream cheese, cubed
¾ c. shredded sharp
    Cheddar cheese
¼ t. hot pepper sauce

Bring first 4 ingredients to a boil in a Dutch oven; gradually stir in grits. Return to a boil; cover, reduce heat and simmer, stirring occasionally, 5 to 7 minutes or until thickened. Add cheeses and hot pepper sauce, stirring until cheeses melt. Serve hot. Serves 4.

Holiday Yams

½ c. all-purpose flour
½ c. brown sugar, packed
½ c. quick-cooking oats,
    uncooked
1 t. cinnamon

⅓ c. butter or margarine, melted
2 (17-oz.) cans yams, drained
1 c. cranberries
1½ c. mini marshmallows

It's just not the holiday season without these yams.

Jamie

Combine flour, sugar, oats, cinnamon and butter until mixture resembles coarse crumbs. Measure out one cup, reserving remaining crumb mixture. Toss together reserved crumb mixture, drained yams and cranberries. Place in a greased 8"x8" baking pan. Top with remaining crumb mixture.

Bake, uncovered, at 350 degrees for 35 minutes. Layer marshmallows on top and broil 4 to 5 inches from heat 2 to 3 minutes or until golden. Serves 6 to 8.

Jamie Ruggerio
Orcutt, CA

get ready, get set

Instead of setting up one or two long dining tables, scatter several smaller ones around the room so friends can chat easily.

3-Cheese Pasta Bake

This yummy mac & cheese dish gets a great update with penne pasta and a trio of cheeses.

8-oz. pkg. penne pasta
2 T. butter
2 T. all-purpose flour
1½ c. milk
½ c. half-and-half
1 c. shredded white Cheddar
  cheese

¼ c. grated Parmesan cheese
2 c. shredded Gruyère cheese,
  divided
1 t. salt
¼ t. pepper
pinch of ground nutmeg

Prepare pasta according to package directions.

Meanwhile, melt butter in a saucepan over medium heat. Whisk in flour until smooth; cook, whisking constantly, one minute. Gradually whisk in milk and half-and-half; cook, whisking constantly, 3 to 5 minutes or until thickened. Stir in Cheddar cheese, Parmesan cheese, one cup Gruyère cheese and next 3 ingredients until smooth.

Stir together pasta and cheese mixture; pour into a lightly greased 11"x7" baking pan. Top with remaining one cup Gruyère cheese.

Bake, uncovered, at 350 degrees for 15 minutes or until golden and bubbly. Serves 4.

Fruited Curry Rice Bake

This dish will fill your kitchen with the rich aromas of curry and cinnamon while it cooks.

8¼-oz. can pear halves in juice
8-oz. can pineapple chunks in juice
¼ c. dried apricots, chopped
¼ c. raisins
3 T. brown sugar, packed
1 t. orange zest

2 (14-oz.) cans chicken broth
2 c. converted rice, uncooked
¾ t. curry powder
½ t. salt
⅛ t. cinnamon
½ c. sliced almonds, toasted

Drain pear and pineapple, reserving juices; chop pear halves. Combine chopped pear, pineapple, apricots and next 3 ingredients in a large bowl; toss.

Add enough broth to reserved juices to measure 4 cups. Add broth mixture, rice and next 3 ingredients to fruit mixture; stir well. Pour into a lightly greased 13"x9" baking pan.

Cover and bake at 350 degrees for one hour or until liquid is absorbed and rice is tender. Let stand 5 minutes before serving. Sprinkle with almonds and serve hot. Serves 8.

Cranberry Relish Salad
(pictured on cover)

This salad is softly set and can be spooned out as a relish or cut into squares and served over lettuce leaves.

2 c. boiling water
2 (3-oz.) pkgs. cherry gelatin mix
¾ c. sugar
3 Red Delicious apples, peeled, cored and quartered
3 navel oranges, peeled and sectioned

1 c. pecan halves, toasted
12-oz. pkg. fresh or frozen cranberries
8-oz. can crushed pineapple

Stir boiling water into gelatin mix in a lightly greased 13"x9" baking pan until gelatin mix is completely dissolved. Add sugar, stirring until completely dissolved.

Process apples and oranges in a food processor until chopped; stir into gelatin mixture. Process pecans and cranberries in food processor until chopped; stir into apple mixture.

Drain pineapple in a wire mesh strainer, pressing out juice with the back of a spoon; reserve juice for another use. Add drained pineapple to cranberry mixture, stirring until fruit and nuts are thoroughly distributed in gelatin mixture. Cover and chill 8 hours. Spoon out as a relish or cut into squares. Serves 10.

Lettuce Wedge Salad

4 to 6 slices bacon
1 onion, sliced
1 c. buttermilk
½ c. sour cream
1-oz. pkg. ranch salad
    dressing mix

¼ c. fresh basil, chopped
2 cloves garlic
1 head iceberg lettuce,
    cut into 4 wedges
Optional: shredded fresh basil

Who can resist a simple iceberg wedge, especially when it's icy cold?

Jo Ann

Cook bacon in a large skillet over medium heat until crisp; remove bacon and drain on paper towels, reserving one tablespoon drippings in skillet. Crumble bacon and set aside.

Sauté onion in hot drippings in skillet over medium heat 10 minutes or until tender and lightly browned. Remove from heat; cool.

Process onion, buttermilk and next 4 ingredients in a blender or food processor until smooth, stopping to scrape down sides.

Top each lettuce wedge with dressing; sprinkle with bacon and top with shredded basil, if desired. Serves 4.

Note: You can make the dressing ahead and store it in the refrigerator. The chilled dressing will have a thicker consistency.

Jo Ann
Gooseberry Patch

Tempting Caesar Salad

1 clove garlic, cut in half
4 anchovy fillets
¾ c. extra-virgin olive oil
6 T. lemon juice
1 t. pepper
½ t. salt

¼ c. red wine vinegar
½ c. egg substitute
1 head romaine lettuce, torn into
   pieces
1 c. grated Parmesan cheese

Rub a wooden salad bowl with cut sides of garlic. Place anchovies in bowl; mash with a fork. Add olive oil and next 4 ingredients; stir well. Whisk egg substitute into mixture. Add lettuce; toss well. Sprinkle with cheese and Croutons. Serves 4.

Croutons:

3 T. olive oil
1 clove garlic, crushed

1 c. day-old French bread,
   cut into cubes

Heat oil and garlic in a large skillet over medium heat. Add bread cubes and sauté 3 to 4 minutes or until golden on all sides. Makes about 16 croutons.

Cashew Salad

1 head lettuce, torn
8-oz. pkg. shredded Swiss
   cheese
1 c. vegetable oil
¾ c. sugar
⅓ c. white vinegar
salt to taste

1 t. mustard
1 t. onion, grated
1 T. poppy seed
1 c. cashews
1 c. croutons
Optional: additional croutons

Toss together lettuce and Swiss cheese in a medium serving bowl. Whisk together oil, sugar, vinegar, salt, mustard, onion and poppy seed. To serve, toss together cashews, croutons, dressing and lettuce mixture. Garnish with additional croutons, if desired. Serves 6 to 8.

Kate Saunier
Grand Rapids, MI

Spinach-Pecan Salad

1 T. butter or margarine
1 T. brown sugar, packed
½ c. pecan halves
7-oz. pkg. baby spinach, washed
1 Granny Smith apple, cored and
    thinly sliced

½ c. crumbled blue cheese
3 T. olive oil
2 T. white vinegar
⅛ t. salt
⅛ t. pepper

The combination of flavors in this salad makes it a favorite!

Vickie

Melt butter and sugar in a small skillet over low heat, stirring constantly. Add pecan halves; cook 2 to 3 minutes, turning to coat. Remove coated pecans from skillet and cool on wax paper.

Toss spinach, apple, cheese and pecans in a serving bowl. Whisk together oil, vinegar, salt and pepper; drizzle over salad, tossing gently to coat. Serves 4.

Vickie
Gooseberry Patch

glass milk bottles

Antique bottles make fun containers for serving salad dressings. Fill each with a different variety of dressing and set them around the table, or place filled bottles in a wire milk carrier...clever!

Layered Cornbread & Turkey Salad

(pictured on page 146)

Smoked turkey, Swiss cheese, vegetables, crumbled cornbread and crisp bacon make a colorful layered salad to serve in a clear bowl or dish.

6-oz. pkg. buttermilk
    cornbread mix
12-oz. bottle Parmesan-
    peppercorn salad dressing
½ c. mayonnaise
¼ c. buttermilk
9-oz. pkg. romaine lettuce,
    shredded
2½ c. cooked smoked turkey,
    chopped

2 yellow peppers, chopped
2 tomatoes, seeded and chopped
1 red onion, chopped
1 c. celery, diced
2 c. shredded Swiss cheese
10 slices bacon, crisply cooked
    and crumbled
Garnish: 2 green onions, sliced

Prepare cornbread according to package directions; cool and crumble. Set aside.

Stir together salad dressing, mayonnaise and buttermilk until blended.

Layer half each of crumbled cornbread, shredded lettuce and remaining ingredients except garnish in a large glass bowl; spoon half of dressing mixture evenly over top. Repeat layers, ending with dressing mixture. Cover and chill at least 8 hours or up to 24 hours. Sprinkle with green onions just before serving. Serves 6.

Sweet Pineapple Coleslaw

1 head cabbage, finely shredded
2 carrots, peeled and shredded
20-oz. can pineapple chunks,
    well drained
½ c. red onion, chopped
½ c. mayonnaise
⅓ c. frozen whipped topping,
    thawed

2 T. sugar
2 T. fresh cilantro, chopped
½ t. hot pepper sauce
½ c. chopped pecans, toasted
Optional: fresh cilantro sprigs

Combine shredded cabbage, carrot, pineapple and red onion in a large bowl. Combine mayonnaise, whipped topping, sugar, chopped cilantro and hot pepper sauce, stirring gently. Add to cabbage mixture; toss gently.

Cover and chill coleslaw one to 2 hours. Sprinkle with toasted pecans just before serving. Serve with a slotted spoon. Garnish with fresh cilantro sprigs, if desired. Serves 6.

potluck pointer

When toting a salad to a get-together, keep it chilled by placing the salad bowl in a larger bowl that is filled with crushed ice.

Apple-Broccoli Salad

Apple-Broccoli Salad

Chock-full of raisins, pecans and bacon, this yummy salad gets coated in a creamy dressing.

4 c. broccoli flowerets
½ c. raisins
½ c. chopped pecans, toasted
6 slices bacon, crisply cooked
    and crumbled

2 Red Delicious apples, diced
1 red onion, chopped
1 c. mayonnaise
½ c. sugar
2 T. cider vinegar

Combine first 6 ingredients in a large bowl. Combine mayonnaise, sugar and vinegar; add to broccoli mixture, stirring to coat. Cover and chill. Serves 6.

Roasted Sweet Potato Salad

Serve this salad chilled or at room temperature. Tossed in rosemary-honey vinaigrette, these golden potatoes come alive with flavor.

4 sweet potatoes, peeled and
    cubed
2 T. olive oil, divided
¼ c. honey
3 T. white wine vinegar

2 T. fresh rosemary, chopped
½ t. salt
½ t. pepper
2 cloves garlic, minced
Optional: fresh rosemary sprig

Coat a large roasting pan with non-stick vegetable spray; toss together potatoes and one tablespoon oil in pan.

Bake, uncovered, at 450 degrees for 45 to 55 minutes or until potatoes are tender and roasted, stirring after 20 minutes.

Whisk together remaining one tablespoon oil, honey and next 5 ingredients. Transfer warm potatoes to a large serving bowl; add dressing and toss gently. Cool. Garnish with a fresh rosemary sprig, if desired. Serves 6 to 8.

Fresh Corn Salad

Use Silver Queen or another sweet corn variety for this sugary-sweet salad with an oil and vinegar dressing. Using corn freshly cut from the cob yields the sweetest kernels.

6 ears white or yellow corn,
    husks removed
¼ c. sugar
¼ c. cider vinegar
¼ c. olive oil
½ t. salt

½ t. pepper
1 red onion, diced
1 red pepper, diced
¼ c. fresh parsley, coarsely
    chopped

Cook corn in boiling salted water in a large stockpot 3 to 4 minutes; drain. Plunge corn into ice water to stop the cooking process; drain. Cut kernels from cobs.

Whisk together sugar and next 4 ingredients in a large bowl; add corn, onion, pepper and parsley, tossing to coat. Cover and chill at least 2 hours. Makes 6 cups.

a new twist

Use old serving dishes in a new way for a fresh look. Handed-down cream-and-sugar sets can hold sauces, bread sticks can be arranged in gravy boats and a trifle dish can make a great salad bowl.

Chocolate Bread, page 201

bountiful breads

Fill your home with the aroma of freshly baked bread throughout the year with these wonderful recipes. Try yummy Melt-in-Your-Mouth Rolls (page 192) for any special occasion. On Christmas morning, wake up to Sticky Bun Biscuits (page 205)...they're perfect with a fresh cup of coffee. Celebrate fall with a big batch of Autumn Apple Cakes (page 213) on Halloween morning. Enjoy these and other scrumptious recipes to fit your holiday needs.

Barley Quick Bread

2 c. all-purpose flour
½ c. pearled barley, uncooked
1 t. salt
1 t. sugar

1 t. baking powder
½ t. baking soda
1 c. buttermilk
¼ c. butter, melted

Mix together first 6 ingredients; stir in buttermilk. Turn dough out onto a lightly floured surface; knead. Roll dough into an oval shape, ½- to ¾-inch thick. Score dough with a knife and prick with a fork; place on a lightly greased and floured baking sheet. Bake at 375 degrees for 15 to 25 minutes. Cool on a wire rack and brush with melted butter. Serves 4 to 6.

Sherry Saarinen
Hancock, MI

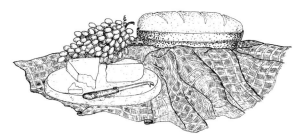

did you know?

Before the introduction of coins, the Egyptians gave loaves of bread as payment for their debts. (This gives new meaning to the word "dough"!)

Dakota Bread

1 pkg. active dry yeast
½ c. warm water
½ c. cottage cheese
¼ c. honey
1 egg
2 T. oil
1 t. salt
2¼ c. bread flour, divided

½ c. whole-wheat flour
¼ c. wheat germ, toasted
¼ c. rye flour
¼ c. long-cooking oats,
    uncooked
2 T. cornmeal
1 egg white, beaten
2 T. sunflower seeds

Combine yeast and warm water (110 to 115 degrees) in a small bowl; let stand 5 minutes. In a large bowl, combine cottage cheese, honey, egg, oil and salt. Beat at medium speed with an electric mixer until blended. Add yeast mixture and 2 cups bread flour, beating until smooth. Gradually stir in whole-wheat flour, wheat germ, rye flour and oats. Add enough remaining bread flour to make a soft dough. Knead dough on a lightly floured surface until smooth and elastic. Place in a greased bowl; cover and let rise one hour or until doubled in bulk. Punch dough down. Shape into one round loaf and place in a pie plate coated with non-stick vegetable spray and sprinkled with cornmeal. Cover with greased plastic wrap and let dough rise again until doubled in bulk. Brush with egg white and sprinkle with sunflower seeds. Bake at 350 degrees for 35 to 40 minutes. Cool on a wire rack. Serves 6 to 8.

Margaret Scoresby
Mosinee, WI

Mom always has this hearty bread waiting in the cupboard when we visit. It's named for all the good grains in it, which are grown in the Dakotas.

Margaret

Whole-Wheat Popovers

Also called Laplanders and puff pops, popovers are considered an
Americanized version of England's Yorkshire pudding.

½ c. all-purpose flour

½ c. whole-wheat flour

¼ t. salt

1 c. 2% reduced-fat milk

2 eggs

2 egg whites

1 T. vegetable oil

Combine first 3 ingredients in a medium bowl. Whisk together milk and next 3 ingredients. Whisk milk mixture into flour mixture, whisking until smooth.

Place popover pan or 6 (8-ounce) custard cups heavily coated with non-stick vegetable spray on a baking sheet. Place in a 425-degree oven 3 minutes or until hot. Remove baking sheet from oven and fill cups half full with batter.

Bake at 425 degrees for 30 minutes. Turn oven off; remove pan from oven. Cut a small slit in top of each popover; return to oven. Let popovers stand in closed oven 3 minutes. Serve immediately. Makes 6 popovers.

Melt-in-Your-Mouth Rolls

*These rolls are
the perfect
accompaniment
to any meal!*

Jerilyn

¾ c. plus 1 t. sugar, divided
½ c. warm water
2 T. active dry yeast
1 c. butter-flavored shortening
1 c. boiling water

1 c. cold water
4 eggs, beaten
2 t. salt
8 c. all-purpose flour, divided

Dissolve one teaspoon sugar in warm water (110 to 115 degrees); sprinkle yeast over it and set aside. Blend shortening and remaining ¾ cup sugar; stir in boiling water. Add cold water, yeast mixture, eggs and salt; mix well. Add flour, 4 cups at a time; mix well. Cover and let dough rise one hour.

Divide dough into thirds. Roll each third into a circle; cut each into 12 wedges. Roll up each wedge crescent-roll style. Cover with plastic wrap that has been sprayed with non-stick vegetable spray; let rise another hour. Bake on ungreased baking sheets at 350 degrees for 15 to 18 minutes. Makes 3 dozen.

Jerilyn Anderson
Provo, UT

brush of herb sprigs

Be sure to place warm melted butter on the table for guests to brush over vegetables or rolls. Make a natural butter brush by bundling sprigs of fresh herbs, such as thyme, oregano, parsley or rosemary, then binding them together with jute.

Herbed Fan Dinner Rolls

When baked, the layers of the roll spread out to mimic a fan.

¼ c. butter or margarine, melted
½ t. dried Italian seasoning

11-oz. pkg. refrigerated bread
dough

Combine butter and Italian seasoning, stirring well. Roll dough into a 13" square. Cut into 4 equal strips. Stack strips on top of each other. Cut strips crosswise into 6 equal stacks. Place each stack, cut side up, in a greased muffin cup; brush with butter mixture. Cover and let rise in a warm place (85 degrees), free from drafts, 25 minutes or until doubled in bulk. Bake at 375 degrees for 22 to 25 minutes or until golden. Brush with butter mixture again, if desired. Makes 6 rolls.

make ahead tip

Place dough pieces in muffin cups; brush with butter mixture. Cover and freeze. Thaw, covered, in a warm place 2 hours or until doubled in bulk. Bake as directed.

Pimento Cheese Biscuits

1 c. shredded sharp Cheddar
   cheese
2¼ c. self-rising soft-wheat flour
½ c. chilled butter, cut into
   ¼-inch-thick slices

1 c. buttermilk
4-oz. jar diced pimento, drained
additional self-rising soft-wheat
   flour
2 T. butter, melted

Combine shredded cheese and 2¼ cups flour in a large bowl.

Sprinkle butter slices over flour-cheese mixture; toss gently. Cut butter into flour with a pastry blender until crumbly and mixture resembles small peas. Cover and chill 10 minutes.

Combine buttermilk and diced pimento; add buttermilk mixture to flour mixture, stirring just until dry ingredients are moistened.

Turn dough out onto a lightly floured surface; knead 3 or 4 times, gradually adding additional flour as needed. With floured hands, press or pat dough into a ¾-inch-thick rectangle (about 9"x5"). Sprinkle top of dough with additional flour. Fold dough over onto itself in 3 sections, starting with one short end. (Fold dough rectangle as if folding a letter-size piece of paper.) Repeat procedure 2 more times, beginning with pressing into a ¾-inch-thick dough rectangle (about 9"x5").

Press or pat dough to ½-inch thickness on a lightly floured surface; cut with a 2-inch round cutter; place, side by side, on a parchment paper-lined or lightly greased 15"x10" jelly-roll pan. (Dough rounds should touch.)

Bake at 450 degrees for 13 to 15 minutes or until lightly golden. Remove from oven and brush with 2 tablespoons melted butter. Makes 2½ dozen.

Parsley Biscuits

2 c. all-purpose flour
1 T. baking powder
½ t. salt
3 T. fresh parsley, chopped

zest of 1 lemon
½ c. shortening
½ c. milk
¼ c. whipping cream

In a large mixing bowl, combine flour, baking powder and salt; add parsley and lemon zest. Using a pastry cutter or 2 knives, cut in shortening until mixture resembles oatmeal. Add milk and cream; blend until mixture forms a ball. Place dough on a lightly floured surface and knead 5 times. Roll out dough to ½-inch thickness and cut out biscuits. Place on lightly greased baking sheets and bake at 425 degrees for 15 minutes or until golden. Makes 8 (2½-inch) biscuits.

Jo Ann
Gooseberry Patch

Broccoli Cornbread

10-oz. pkg. frozen chopped
   broccoli, thawed
8½-oz. pkg. corn muffin mix
4 eggs, lightly beaten

1 c. cottage cheese
½ c. butter or margarine, melted
1 onion, minced
1 t. salt

Drain broccoli, pressing between paper towels. Combine muffin mix and next 5 ingredients; stir. Add broccoli. Pour into a greased 13"x9" baking pan; bake at 400 degrees for 20 to 25 minutes or until golden. Cool; cut into squares. Serves 12.

Savory Sausage-Swiss Muffins

Store any leftover muffins in the refrigerator. Then, reheat leftovers in the microwave; microwave one muffin on high 20 to 30 seconds.

½ lb. mild or spicy ground pork
    sausage
1¾ c. biscuit baking mix
½ c. shredded Swiss cheese

¾ t. ground sage
¼ t. dried thyme
1 egg, lightly beaten
½ c. milk

Brown sausage in a skillet over medium heat, stirring until it crumbles. Drain well.

Combine sausage, biscuit mix and next 3 ingredients in a bowl; make a well in center of mixture.

Combine egg and milk; add to dry ingredients, stirring just until dry ingredients are moistened. Spoon batter into greased muffin cups, filling cups ⅔ full. Bake at 375 degrees for 22 minutes or until golden. Serve warm. Makes one dozen.

the right mix

For the most tender loaves and muffins, don't overmix…combine the batter until just moistened. A few lumps won't matter.

Jack-o'-Lantern Bread

Follow package directions for thawing bread dough. If making ahead, wrap cooled bread airtight and keep at room temperature up to one day or freeze to store longer. Reheat (thaw, if frozen), loosely covered with foil, in a 350-degree oven 10 to 15 minutes or until warm.

2 (1-lb.) loaves frozen bread dough, thawed	1 T. beaten egg 1½ t. milk

Place the loaves in a bowl. Cover bowl with plastic wrap and let rise until doubled, 45 minutes to one hour. Punch dough down, knead loaves together in bowl and shape into a ball.

Transfer ball to a greased 15"x12" baking sheet. With greased hands or a lightly floured rolling pin, flatten ball into a 13"x11" oval. Cut out eyes, nose and mouth; openings should be at least 1½ to 2 inches wide. (To make small loaves, divide dough into 4 equal pieces and roll into 6"x4" ovals; eye, nose and mouth openings should be at least one to 1½ inches wide.) Lift out cut-out dough and bake on another pan or use for decoration.

Cover the shaped dough lightly with plastic wrap and let rise until puffy, about 20 minutes. Mix egg with milk; brush over dough. Bake at 350 degrees for 30 to 35 minutes or until golden. Cool on a wire rack. Serve warm or cool. Serves 10 to 12.

Vickie
Gooseberry Patch

Kids love these! Marinara sauce is great for dipping.
Vickie

Best-Ever Soft Pretzels

1 env. active dry yeast
1½ c. warm water
1 T. sugar
2 t. salt

4 c. all-purpose flour
1 egg yolk
1 T. water
¼ c. coarse salt

There's nothing like these warm pretzels sprinkled with salt!

Vickie

In a large bowl, dissolve yeast in warm water (110 to 115 degrees). Stir in sugar and salt until dissolved. Add flour; mix well. Turn dough out onto a floured surface; knead 5 minutes. Divide dough into 16 equal pieces. Roll into thin strips; shape into pretzels. Place on a well-greased baking sheet. Beat egg yolk with water; brush on pretzels. Sprinkle with salt; bake at 425 degrees for 15 to 20 minutes or until golden. Makes 16 pretzels.

Vickie
Gooseberry Patch

Chocolate Bread
(pictured on page 186)

1¼ c. milk
½ c. water
1 env. active dry yeast
4½ c. all-purpose flour, divided
½ c. baking cocoa
¼ c. sugar

1 t. salt
1 egg
2 T. butter, softened
2 (4-oz.) semi-sweet chocolate
   bars, chopped
1½ T. turbinado sugar

Heat milk and water until warm (110 to 115 degrees). Combine with yeast in a large bowl; whisk until smooth. Let stand 5 minutes. Stir 2 cups flour, cocoa, sugar and salt into yeast mixture; beat at medium speed with an electric mixer until smooth. Beat in egg, butter and 2 cups flour until a soft dough forms.

Turn dough out onto a floured surface; knead until smooth (about 6 minutes), adding remaining ½ cup flour, one tablespoon at a time as needed, to prevent dough from sticking. Fold in chopped chocolate during last minute of kneading.

Place dough in a large, lightly greased bowl, turning to coat top. Cover with plastic wrap; let rise in a warm place (85 degrees), free from drafts, one hour and 40 minutes or until doubled in bulk.

Punch down dough. Divide dough in half; gently shape each portion into an 8"x4" oval. Place dough in 2 lightly greased 8½"x4½" loaf pans. Cover and let rise 1½ hours or until doubled in bulk.

Sprinkle loaves with turbinado sugar. Bake at 375 degrees for 25 minutes or until loaves sound hollow when tapped. Remove from pans. Let cool on a wire rack. Makes 2 loaves.

Orange Coffee Rolls

1 env. active dry yeast
¼ c. warm water
1 c. sugar, divided
2 eggs
½ c. sour cream
¼ c. plus 2 T. butter, melted

1 t. salt
2¾ to 3 c. all-purpose flour
2 T. butter, melted and divided
1 c. flaked coconut, toasted and divided
2 T. orange zest

Combine yeast and warm water (110 to 115 degrees) in a large bowl; let stand 5 minutes. Add ¼ cup sugar and next 4 ingredients; beat at medium speed with an electric mixer until blended. Gradually stir in enough flour to make a soft dough. Turn dough out onto a well-floured surface; knead until smooth and elastic (about 5 minutes). Place in a well-greased bowl, turning to grease top. Cover and let rise in a warm place (85 degrees), free from drafts, 1½ hours or until doubled in bulk. Punch dough down and divide in half. Roll one portion of dough into a 12-inch circle; brush with one tablespoon melted butter. Combine remaining ¾ cup sugar, ¾ cup coconut and orange zest; sprinkle half of coconut mixture over dough. Cut into 12 wedges; roll up each wedge, beginning at wide end. Place in a greased 13"x9" baking pan, point side down. Repeat with remaining dough, butter and coconut mixture. Cover and let rise in a warm place, free from drafts, 45 minutes or until doubled in bulk.

Bake at 350 degrees for 25 to 30 minutes or until golden. (Cover with aluminum foil after 15 minutes to prevent excessive browning, if necessary.) Spoon warm Glaze over warm rolls; sprinkle with remaining ¼ cup coconut. Makes 2 dozen.

Glaze:

¾ c. sugar
½ c. sour cream

¼ c. butter
2 t. orange juice

Combine all ingredients in a small saucepan; bring to a boil. Boil 3 minutes, stirring occasionally. Let cool slightly. Makes 1⅓ cups.

Sweet Potato Biscuits

These taste great!

Ruth

¾ c. sweet potatoes, cooked, peeled, mashed and chilled
½ c. butter, melted and cooled
¼ c. brown sugar, packed
½ c. milk
2 c. all-purpose flour
1½ t. baking powder
½ t. salt

In a large bowl, combine sweet potatoes, butter and brown sugar. Stir in milk and blend until smooth. Sift together dry ingredients and add to sweet potato mixture.

Turn dough out onto a lightly floured surface and knead 6 times. Use a floured rolling pin to roll out dough to ½-inch thickness. Cut out with a 2-inch round cutter. Place biscuits one inch apart on lightly greased baking sheets. Bake at 400 degrees for 15 minutes or until golden. Makes about 1½ dozen.

Ruth Gomez
Toledo, OH

Sticky Bun Biscuits

For the ultimate breakfast, add coffee and fresh fruit.

1 c. brown sugar, packed
¾ c. butter or margarine
½ c. light corn syrup
1 c. pecans, coarsely chopped

3 c. self-rising flour
¼ c. sugar
¾ c. shortening
1 c. milk

Combine first 3 ingredients in a saucepan; cook over medium heat, stirring constantly, until melted and smooth. Pour mixture into a greased 13"x9" baking pan; sprinkle with pecans. Set aside.

Combine flour and sugar; cut in shortening with a pastry blender or 2 knives until mixture is crumbly. Add milk, stirring until dry ingredients are moistened. Turn dough out onto a lightly floured surface; knead 4 or 5 times.

Roll out dough to ¾-inch thickness; cut with a 2-inch biscuit cutter. Place biscuits over brown sugar mixture in pan. Bake at 400 degrees for 18 to 20 minutes or until done. Remove from oven and let stand 5 minutes. Invert onto a serving platter; remove pan. Spoon any additional brown sugar glaze over biscuits; serve immediately. Makes 1½ dozen.

breakfast in bed

Make someone feel extra special...serve them breakfast in bed! Fill a tray with breakfast goodies, the morning paper and a bright blossom tucked into a vase.

Sugar-Topped Muffins

Sugar-Topped Muffins

Enjoy these warm muffins for a real treat!

18¼-oz. pkg. white cake mix
1 c. milk
2 eggs
½ t. nutmeg
⅓ c. sugar
½ t. cinnamon
¼ c. butter, melted

Blend cake mix, milk, eggs and nutmeg at low speed with an electric mixer until just moistened; beat at high speed 2 minutes. Fill paper-lined muffin cups ⅔ full. Bake at 350 degrees until golden, about 15 to 18 minutes. Cool 5 minutes. Combine sugar and cinnamon on a small plate. Brush muffin tops with butter; roll in sugar and cinnamon mixture. Serve warm. Makes 2 dozen.

Streusel Cran-Orange Muffins

1½ c. all-purpose flour
1 t. baking powder
½ t. baking soda
½ t. salt
1 egg, lightly beaten
½ c. cranberry-orange relish
1 t. orange zest
⅓ c. orange juice
¼ c. brown sugar, packed
¼ c. butter or margarine, melted
⅓ c. chopped pecans
¼ c. brown sugar, packed
½ t. cinnamon

Combine first 4 ingredients in a large bowl; make a well in center of mixture. Combine egg and next 5 ingredients; add to dry ingredients, stirring just until moistened. Spoon into greased muffin cups, filling ⅔ full.

Combine pecans, brown sugar and cinnamon; sprinkle over muffins. Bake at 400 degrees for 15 minutes or until golden. Remove from pans immediately. Makes one dozen.

Lemony Poppy Seed Bread

These mini loaves wrapped in pretty plastic wrap make welcome gifts any time of the year.

Vicki

18¼-oz. pkg. lemon cake mix
3.4-oz. pkg. instant lemon
    pudding mix
4 eggs
1 c. water
½ c. oil
1 to 2 t. poppy seed

Blend together first 5 ingredients, mixing well. Stir in poppy seed. Pour into 2 lightly greased and floured 8"x4" loaf pans; bake at 350 degrees for 45 minutes. Cool in pans 10 minutes. Serves 16.

Vicki Moats
Wyoming, IL

Harvest Pumpkin Bread

Dress up this bread with raisins or walnuts, if you like.

2 c. all-purpose flour, divided
1 c. brown sugar, packed
1 t. cinnamon
¼ t. nutmeg
⅛ t. ground cloves
1 T. baking powder
¼ t. baking soda
¼ t. salt
1 c. canned pumpkin
½ c. milk
⅓ c. butter or margarine,
    softened
2 eggs

Combine one cup flour, brown sugar, cinnamon, nutmeg, cloves, baking powder, baking soda and salt in a mixing bowl. Add pumpkin, milk, butter and eggs and beat at low speed with an electric mixer until blended; increase speed to high and beat 2 minutes. Gradually add remaining flour and beat until well mixed. Pour batter into a greased 9"x5" loaf pan and bake for 60 to 65 minutes. Makes one loaf.

Cream Cheese Braids

The perfect food for Christmas morning...beautiful braided bread drizzled with icing.

16-oz. pkg. hot roll mix
8-oz. pkg. cream cheese,
   softened
⅓ c. sugar
2 t. vanilla extract, divided

2 egg yolks, divided
⅛ t. salt
1 c. powdered sugar
1 T. milk

Prepare dough from hot roll mix according to package directions, using yeast packet. Turn dough out onto a lightly floured surface and knead 4 to 5 times. Divide dough in half; roll each portion of dough into a 12"x8" rectangle.

Beat cream cheese, sugar, one teaspoon vanilla, one egg yolk and salt until blended. Spread half of cream cheese mixture lengthwise down center of each dough rectangle.

Working with one dough rectangle at a time, cut 9 (3-inch-long) deep slits into each long side of dough. Fold strips over cream cheese filling, alternating sides and making a braid. Pinch ends to seal and tuck under, if desired. Carefully place loaves on greased baking sheets.

Cover and let rise in a warm place (85 degrees), free from drafts, 30 minutes. Brush tops with beaten egg yolk. Bake at 375 degrees for 15 minutes or until golden.

Combine powdered sugar, milk and one teaspoon vanilla, stirring well; drizzle over warm loaves. Makes 2 (12-inch) loaves.

midnight breakfast

If you're hosting a sleepover, the kids will likely stay up late giggling. Plan to throw a mini breakfast at midnight! Set up a room filled with games, movies and lots of yummy things to eat...breakfast rolls, muffins and doughnuts.

Ginger Scones

2¾ c. all-purpose flour
2 t. baking powder
½ t. salt
½ c. sugar

¾ c. butter
⅓ c. chopped crystallized ginger
1 c. milk

Combine first 4 ingredients in a large bowl; cut butter into flour mixture with a pastry blender until crumbly. Stir in ginger. Add milk, stirring just until dry ingredients are moistened. Turn dough out onto a lightly floured surface and knead 10 to 15 times. Pat or roll dough to ¾-inch thickness; shape into a round and cut dough into 8 wedges. Place wedges on a lightly greased baking sheet.

Bake at 400 degrees for 18 to 22 minutes or until scones are barely golden. Cool slightly on a wire rack. Makes 8 scones.

Vickie
Gooseberry Patch

Top these yummy scones with sweetened whipped cream!

Vickie

morning cheer

Tuck cheery blossoms inside lots of 1950s-era egg cups and scatter them on the breakfast table. They'll make everyone feel perky even before the orange juice is served!

Mothers' Day

Almond French Toast

6 (1-inch-thick) slices French
    bread
4 eggs
½ c. milk
1 T. sugar
1 t. almond extract

½ t. vanilla extract
Optional: 2 T. almond liqueur
3 T. butter
½ c. sliced almonds, toasted
powdered sugar
maple syrup, warmed

Arrange French bread slices in a 13"x9" baking pan.

Whisk together eggs, next 4 ingredients and, if desired, liqueur; pour over bread. Let stand 5 minutes, turning once. Cover and chill 8 hours, if desired.

Place butter in a 15"x10" jelly-roll pan; place pan in 400-degree oven until butter is melted. Place soaked bread slices in melted butter in pan.

Bake at 400 degrees for 15 minutes; turn each slice and bake 8 to 10 more minutes or until golden. Sprinkle with almonds and powdered sugar. Serve with maple syrup. Serves 3.

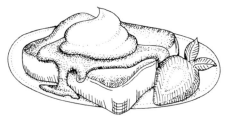

special topping

French toast is scrumptious topped with homemade whipped cream. For the fluffiest whipped cream possible, always make sure the bowl and beaters are chilled.

Autumn Apple Cakes

These pancakes are made with chunky applesauce in the batter. They taste great with a topping of sweetened applesauce or apple butter.

2 eggs, beaten
1 c. milk
1 c. chunky applesauce
¾ c. light brown sugar, packed

2 c. biscuit baking mix
1 t. cinnamon
4 to 5 T. oil, divided

Combine first 4 ingredients in a large bowl, stirring with a whisk until sugar dissolves. Combine biscuit baking mix and cinnamon; add to applesauce mixture. Stir with a wire whisk just until moistened.

Heat a 9-inch skillet or griddle over medium-low heat until hot. Heat one tablespoon oil in skillet. Pour about ¼ cup batter for each pancake into skillet; cook 3½ to 4 minutes or until tops are covered with bubbles and edges look cooked. Turn and cook other side.

Remove pancakes to a serving platter; keep warm. Repeat procedure with remaining batter, adding one tablespoon oil to skillet per batch. Makes 18 pancakes.

Jo Ann
Gooseberry Patch

Yum! These are perfect on a fall morning.

Jo Ann

Blueberry 'n' Cheese Coffee Cake

This moist blueberry cream cheese cake with a lemon-sugar topping is special enough for company.

½ c. plus 2 T. butter, softened
   and divided
1¾ c. sugar, divided
2 eggs
2½ c. all-purpose flour, divided
1 t. baking powder
1 t. salt

¾ c. milk
¼ c. water
2 c. fresh blueberries
8-oz. pkg. cream cheese, cut
   into ¼-inch cubes
2 T. lemon zest

Beat ½ cup butter at medium speed with an electric mixer until creamy; gradually add 1¼ cups sugar, beating well. Add eggs, one at a time, beating until blended after each addition.

Combine 2 cups flour, baking powder and salt; stir well. Combine milk and water; stir well. Add flour mixture to butter mixture alternately with milk mixture, beginning and ending with flour mixture. Mix at low speed after each addition until mixture is blended. Gently stir in blueberries and cream cheese. Pour batter into a greased 9"x9" baking pan.

Combine ½ cup flour, ½ cup sugar, lemon zest and 2 tablespoons butter ; stir well with a fork. Sprinkle mixture over batter. Bake at 375 degrees for 55 minutes or until golden. Serve warm or let cool completely on a wire rack. Serves 16.

did you know?

The American tradition of serving coffee and sweet cake along with gossip actually evolved from the tradition of English tea.

Patriotic Cupcakes, page 227

divine
desserts

What's one of the best things about holiday get-togethers? The dessert table!
From cakes and pies to cookies and ice cream, this melt-in-your-mouth
collection of delicious desserts is sure to be a hit. Enjoy a sweet ending
to your Easter brunch with rich Caramel Cake (page 221), serve Perfect
Pecan Pie (page 241) after Thanksgiving dinner and
ring in the New Year with decadent
Bread Pudding (page 249). Host a
Christmas caroling party and pass
around plates of Sugar Cookies
(page 253) and Chocolate-Caramel
Thumbprints (page 255)...just be
sure to save some for Santa!

Warm Turtle Cake

A cake that reminds me of the boxes of chocolate-covered turtles that my dad used to bring home for us when we were little!

Laurie

18¼-oz. pkg. Swiss chocolate cake mix
½ c. plus ⅓ c. evaporated milk, divided
¾ c. butter, melted

14-oz. pkg. caramels, unwrapped
1 c. chopped pecans
¾ c. chocolate chips

Beat cake mix, ⅓ cup evaporated milk and melted butter at medium speed with an electric mixer 2 minutes. Pour half of mixture into a greased 11"x7" baking pan. Bake at 350 degrees for 6 minutes. In a double boiler or microwave, melt caramels in the remaining ½ cup evaporated milk. Drizzle over cake. Sprinkle pecans and chocolate chips over caramel mixture. Use a wet knife to spread the remaining cake mixture over the pecan pieces and chocolate chips. Bake at 350 degrees for 18 minutes. Serves 12.

Laurie Benham
Playas, NM

extra special

For a little something extra on cakes and brownies, try topping with chopped candy bars. Make chopping a breeze when you wrap them in plastic and freeze for 10 to 15 minutes beforehand.

Mom's Special Occasion Cherry Cake

A perfect dessert to enjoy with your sweetheart!

2¼ c. cake flour
2½ t. baking powder
¼ t. salt
½ c. shortening
1⅓ c. sugar
3 egg whites

⅔ c. milk
10-oz. jar maraschino cherries, drained with juice reserved
½ c. chopped walnuts
4-oz. jar maraschino cherries with stems

Combine flour, baking powder and salt in a small bowl; set aside. Beat shortening in a large bowl 30 seconds; beat in sugar. Gradually add egg whites, beating well after each addition; set aside. Whisk together milk and ¼ cup reserved cherry juice; add alternately with flour mixture to sugar mixture, mixing well. Fold in nuts and drained cherries; divide batter evenly between 2 lightly greased and floured 8" round cake pans. Bake at 350 degrees for 25 to 30 minutes; cool on a wire rack 10 minutes. Remove from pans to cool completely; spread Butter Frosting between layers and on the top and sides of cake. Decorate top with a ring of stemmed cherries. Serves 8 to 10.

Butter Frosting:

¾ c. butter, softened
6 c. powdered sugar, divided
⅓ c. milk

¼ t. salt
1½ t. vanilla extract
4 to 6 drops red food coloring

Beat butter until fluffy; mix in 3 cups powdered sugar. Gradually blend in milk, salt and vanilla; add remaining 3 cups powdered sugar, mixing well. Stir in food coloring to desired tint.

Roger Baker
La Rue, OH

Caramel Cake

8-oz. container sour cream
¼ c. milk
1 c. butter, softened
2 c. sugar
4 eggs

2¾ c. all-purpose flour
2 t. baking powder
½ t. salt
1 t. vanilla extract

Combine sour cream and milk.

Beat butter at medium speed with an electric mixer until creamy. Gradually add sugar, beating well. Add eggs, one at a time, beating until blended after each addition.

Combine flour, baking powder and salt; add to butter mixture alternately with sour cream mixture, beginning and ending with flour mixture. Beat at medium-low speed until blended after each addition. Stir in vanilla. Pour batter into 2 greased and floured 9" round cake pans.

Bake at 350 degrees for 30 to 35 minutes or until a toothpick inserted in center comes out clean. Cool in pans on wire racks 10 minutes. Remove from pans to wire racks and let cool one hour or until completely cool. Spread Whipped Cream Caramel Frosting between layers and on top and sides of cake. Serves 8.

Whipped Cream Caramel Frosting:

1 c. butter
2 c. dark brown sugar, packed
¼ c. plus 2 T. whipping cream

2 t. vanilla extract
3¾ c. powdered sugar

Melt butter in a 3-quart saucepan over medium heat. Add brown sugar; bring to a boil, stirring constantly. Stir in whipping cream and vanilla; bring to a boil. Remove from heat; let cool one hour. Transfer frosting to a mixing bowl.

Sift powdered sugar into frosting. Beat at high speed with an electric mixer until creamy and spreading consistency. Makes 3¾ cups.

Fathers' Day

Red Velvet Layer Cake

1 c. butter, softened
2½ c. sugar
6 eggs
3 c. all-purpose flour
3 T. baking cocoa

¼ t. baking soda
8-oz. container sour cream
2 t. vanilla extract
2 (1-oz.) bottles red food
    coloring

Beat butter at medium speed with an electric mixer until creamy. Gradually add sugar, beating until light and fluffy. Add eggs, one at a time, beating just until blended after each addition.

Stir together flour, cocoa and baking soda. Add to butter mixture alternately with sour cream, beginning and ending with flour mixture. Beat at low speed just until blended after each addition. Stir in vanilla; stir in red food coloring. Spoon cake batter into 3 greased and floured 8" round cake pans.

Bake at 350 degrees for 18 to 20 minutes or until a toothpick inserted in center comes out clean. Cool in pans on wire racks 10 minutes. Remove from pans to wire racks; let cool one hour or until completely cool.

Spread 5-Cup Cream Cheese Frosting between layers and on top and sides of cake. Serves 12.

5-Cup Cream Cheese Frosting:

2 (8-oz.) pkgs. cream cheese,
    softened
½ c. butter, softened

2 (16-oz.) pkgs. powdered sugar
2 t. vanilla extract

Beat cream cheese and butter at medium speed with an electric mixer until creamy. Gradually add powdered sugar, beating until fluffy. Stir in vanilla. Makes about 5 cups.

Apple Spice Cake

18¼-oz. pkg. spice cake mix
4 eggs
½ c. oil

1 c. apple juice
3.4-oz. pkg. instant butterscotch
    pudding mix

Combine all ingredients in a large bowl; beat at medium speed with an electric mixer 2 minutes or until blended. Pour batter into a greased and floured 13"x9" baking pan.

Bake at 350 degrees for 35 to 38 minutes or until a toothpick inserted in center comes out clean. Cool cake in pan on a wire rack 30 minutes. Pour Caramel Glaze evenly over cake. Serves 12.

Caramel Glaze:

1 c. light brown sugar, packed
½ c. butter or margarine

½ c. evaporated milk
1 t. vanilla extract

Combine first 3 ingredients in a medium saucepan over medium-high heat; bring to a boil. Boil 3 minutes, stirring constantly. Remove from heat; stir in vanilla. Cool completely. Makes 1¼ cups.

homemade goodness

Add a dollop of homemade whipped cream to pie and cake slices…it's a snap to make and tastes so much better than store-bought. Combine one cup heavy cream with ¼ cup powdered sugar and one teaspoon vanilla extract in a chilled bowl; beat until soft peaks form.

White Christmas Coconut Sheet Cake

18¼-oz. pkg. white cake mix
¾ c. cream of coconut
¼ c. butter, melted
3 eggs
½ c. water
¾ c. lemon curd
4 oz. white chocolate, chopped
½ c. sour cream
1 c. whipping cream
¼ c. powdered sugar
6-oz. pkg. frozen grated coconut, thawed
Optional: maraschino cherries with stems, lemon zest

Combine first 5 ingredients in a large bowl; beat at low speed with an electric mixer one minute. Increase speed to medium and beat 1½ minutes. Spread batter into a greased and floured 13"x9" baking pan.

Bake at 350 degrees for 35 minutes or until a toothpick inserted in center comes out clean. Remove pan to a wire rack; spread lemon curd over hot cake. Let cool completely in pan on wire rack. (Cake will sink slightly in center.)

Microwave white chocolate in a small microwave-safe bowl on high one minute or until melted, stirring after 30 seconds. Stir in sour cream. Cover and chill 30 minutes.

Beat whipping cream and powdered sugar in a large bowl at medium speed until stiff peaks form. Add white chocolate mixture and beat at low speed just until combined. Spread whipped cream topping over cake; sprinkle with coconut. Cover and chill 8 hours. Garnish with maraschino cherries and lemon zest, if desired. Store in refrigerator. Serves 15.

Jo Ann
Gooseberry Patch

Enjoy this sheet cake slathered with lemon curd, whipped cream and plenty of coconut.

Jo Ann

Chocolate-Caramel Sheet Cake

A delicious mixture of two wonderful flavors...chocolate and caramel.

Vickie

1 c. butter
1 c. water
¼ c. baking cocoa
½ c. buttermilk
2 eggs
1 t. baking soda

1 t. vanilla extract
2 c. sugar
2 c. all-purpose flour
½ t. salt
1½ c. pecans, coarsely chopped
     and toasted

Cook first 3 ingredients in a small saucepan over low heat, stirring constantly, until butter melts and mixture is smooth; remove from heat.

Beat buttermilk and next 3 ingredients at medium speed with an electric mixer until smooth; add cocoa mixture, beating until blended.

Combine sugar, flour and salt; gradually add to buttermilk mixture, beating just until blended. Batter will be thin. Line a 15"x10" jelly-roll pan with heavy-duty aluminum foil, allowing several inches to extend over sides. Grease and flour foil. Pour batter into pan. Bake at 350 degrees for 20 to 25 minutes or until a toothpick inserted in center comes out clean. Cool cake completely in pan on a wire rack.

Pour warm Quick Caramel Frosting over cake, spreading evenly to edges of pan. Sprinkle evenly with pecans. Serves 15.

Quick Caramel Frosting:

½ c. butter
½ c. light brown sugar, packed
½ c. dark brown sugar, packed

¼ c. milk
2 c. powdered sugar
1 t. vanilla extract

Bring first 3 ingredients to a boil in a 3½-quart saucepan over medium heat, whisking constantly, about 2 minutes. Stir in milk and bring to a boil; remove from heat. Add powdered sugar and vanilla, stirring with a wooden spoon until smooth. Use immediately. Makes 3 cups.

Vickie
Gooseberry Patch

4th of July

Patriotic Cupcakes
(pictured on page 216)

2 c. sugar
1 c. butter, softened
2 eggs
2 t. lemon juice
1 t. vanilla extract
2½ c. cake flour

½ t. baking soda
1 c. buttermilk
5-Cup Cream Cheese Frosting
  (page 222)
24 mini American flags

Beat sugar and butter at medium speed with an electric mixer until creamy. Add eggs, one at a time, beating until yellow disappears after each addition. Beat in lemon juice and vanilla.

Combine flour and baking soda in a small bowl; add to sugar mixture alternately with buttermilk, beginning and ending with flour mixture. Beat at medium speed just until blended after each addition.

Spoon batter into paper-lined muffin cups, filling ⅔ full.

Bake at 350 degrees for 18 to 22 minutes or until a toothpick inserted in center comes out clean. Cool in pans on a wire rack 10 minutes. Remove cupcakes from pans to wire rack; cool 45 minutes or until completely cool.

Spoon 5-Cup Cream Cheese Frosting into a plastic zipping bag (do not seal). Snip one corner of bag to make a hole (about one inch in diameter). Pipe frosting in little loops onto tops of cupcakes as desired. Insert one flag into top of each cupcake. Makes 2 dozen.

Note: To make ahead, bake and cool cupcakes as directed. Do not frost and decorate. Double-wrap cupcakes in plastic wrap and heavy-duty aluminum foil or place in airtight containers; freeze up to one month.

edible centerpiece

A heaping plate of cookies, bars, cupcakes or cake squares makes a delightful (and delicious) centerpiece at a casual gathering with friends.

Jumbo Chocolate Cupcakes

1 c. butter, softened
½ c. sugar
1 c. light brown sugar, packed
4 eggs
3 (1-oz.) sqs. unsweetened
  baking chocolate, melted
3 (1-oz.) sqs. semi-sweet baking
  chocolate, melted

1 t. vanilla extract
2 c. all-purpose flour
1 t. baking soda
½ t. salt
1 c. buttermilk
12 Christmas-themed cupcake
  toppers

Beat butter at medium speed with an electric mixer until creamy. Gradually add sugars, beating well. Add eggs, one at a time, beating after each addition. Add melted chocolates and vanilla, beating well.

Combine flour, baking soda and salt; add to batter alternately with buttermilk, beginning and ending with flour mixture. Beat at low speed after each addition until blended. Spoon batter into paper-lined jumbo muffin cups, filling ¾ full. Bake at 350 degrees for 30 minutes or until a toothpick inserted in center comes out clean. Cool in pans on wire racks 5 minutes. Remove from pans and cool completely on wire racks 45 minutes. Spread with Thick Chocolate Frosting. Insert one topper into top of each cupcake. Makes one dozen.

Thick Chocolate Frosting:

½ c. butter, softened
16-oz. pkg. powdered sugar
1 c. semi-sweet chocolate
  chips, melted

½ c. whipping cream
2 t. vanilla extract
⅛ t. salt

Beat butter at medium speed with an electric mixer until creamy; gradually add powdered sugar alternately with melted chocolate and whipping cream. Beat at low speed after each addition until blended. Stir in vanilla and salt. Makes 3½ cups.

Pretty Little Cakes

These bite-size cakes make every party a special one.

18¼-oz. pkg. white cake mix
1⅓ c. water
2 T. oil
3 egg whites
2 t. almond extract
10 c. sifted powdered sugar

1 c. water
3 T. light corn syrup
1 t. vanilla or almond extract
Garnish: candied violets or
    flower-shaped candies

Line bottom of a greased 15"x10" jelly-roll pan with wax paper; grease wax paper. In a large bowl, combine cake mix, water, oil, egg whites and almond extract. Pour batter into prepared pan. Bake 18 to 22 minutes or until a toothpick inserted in center comes out clean and top is golden. Cool in pan 10 minutes. Invert cake onto a wire rack and cool completely. Transfer cake to a baking sheet covered with wax paper. Freeze cake 2 hours or until firm. Using a serrated knife, cut away sides of cake to straighten. Cut cake into 2-inch squares. Place squares 2 inches apart on wire racks with wax paper underneath.

For icing, combine powdered sugar and remaining ingredients except garnish in a large saucepan; cook over low heat, stirring constantly, until smooth. Quickly pour warm icing over cake squares, completely covering top and sides. Spoon all excess icing into saucepan; reheat until smooth. (If necessary, add a small amount of water to maintain icing's original consistency.) Continue pouring and reheating icing until all cakes have been iced twice. Garnish each cake with candied violets. Let icing harden completely. Trim any excess icing from bottom edges of each cake square. Store cakes in an airtight container. Makes about 40.

Pumpkin Cake Roll

¾ c. all-purpose flour
2 to 3 t. pumpkin pie spice
1 t. baking powder
½ t. salt
3 eggs
1 c. sugar

⅔ c. canned pumpkin
1 t. lemon juice
1 c. pecans or walnuts, finely
    chopped
powdered sugar

You will have people wanting another piece of this delicious dessert.

Lisa

Combine flour, pumpkin pie spice, baking powder and salt. In a separate bowl, beat eggs at high speed with an electric mixer 5 minutes. Gradually beat in sugar. Stir in pumpkin and lemon juice. Stir in flour mixture. Spread in a greased and floured 15"x10" jelly-roll pan. Sprinkle nuts on top. Bake at 375 degrees for 15 minutes.

Turn out on towel sprinkled with powdered sugar. Starting at narrow end, roll towel and cake together and let cool. Unroll. Spread filling over cake and reroll. Chill. Serve hot Nutmeg Sauce over pumpkin cake roll, if desired. Serves 8 to 10.

Filling:

1 c. powdered sugar
6 oz. cream cheese, softened

4 T. butter, softened
½ t. vanilla extract

Combine all ingredients. Beat until smooth.

Nutmeg Sauce:

1 c. sugar
2 T. all-purpose flour
½ t. nutmeg

2 c. water
1 T. butter
1 T. white or cider vinegar

Combine sugar, flour and nutmeg in a 2-quart saucepan. Add water and stir while heating to a boil. Reduce heat and boil gently 5 minutes. Stir frequently. Remove from heat and stir in butter and vinegar. Makes about 2 cups.

Lisa Murch

Million-Dollar Pound Cake

2 c. butter, softened
3 c. sugar
6 eggs
4 c. all-purpose flour
¾ c. milk

1 t. almond extract
1 t. vanilla extract
Optional: sweetened whipped
    cream, blueberries, sliced
    peaches

Beat butter at medium speed with an electric mixer until light yellow in color and creamy. Gradually add sugar, beating at medium speed until light and fluffy. Add eggs, one at a time, beating just until yellow disappears after each addition.

Add flour to butter mixture alternately with milk, beginning and ending with flour. Beat at low speed just until blended after each addition. (Batter should be smooth.) Stir in extracts. Pour batter into a greased and floured 10" tube pan.

Bake at 300 degrees for one hour and 40 minutes or until a long wooden pick inserted in center comes out clean. Cool in pan on a wire rack 10 to 15 minutes. Remove from pan and cool completely on wire rack. Garnish each serving with whipped cream, blueberries and sliced peaches, if desired. Serves 10 to 12.

vintage finds

Look for vintage pie tins, servers and cake plates at flea markets…add them to your collection or make them part of the gift when sharing a favorite sweet treat.

Cranberry-Ginger Crumble Cake

A pretty cranberry filling and a yummy candied ginger topping will keep you nibbling on this coffee cake.

2 c. fresh or frozen cranberries
2½ c. sugar, divided
1 T. cornstarch
1½ t. lemon zest
¾ c. water
2¾ c. all-purpose flour, divided
¼ c. cold butter, cut into pieces
2.7-oz. jar crystallized ginger, finely chopped (½ c.)
8-oz. pkg. cream cheese, softened
½ c. butter or margarine, softened
2 eggs
1½ t. baking powder
½ t. baking soda
½ t. salt
¼ c. milk
½ t. vanilla extract

Stir together cranberries, 1½ cups sugar, cornstarch and lemon zest in a saucepan; stir in water. Bring to a boil; reduce heat and simmer, uncovered, 25 minutes or until cranberry skins pop and mixture is thickened. Remove from heat; set aside to cool.

Combine ¾ cup flour, ¼ cup sugar and ¼ cup cold butter with a pastry blender or 2 knives until crumbly. Stir in ginger; set aside.

Beat cream cheese and ½ cup softened butter at medium speed with an electric mixer until creamy; gradually add remaining ¾ cup sugar, beating well. Add eggs, one at a time, beating until blended after each addition.

Combine remaining 2 cups flour, baking powder, baking soda and salt; add to cream cheese mixture alternately with milk, beginning and ending with flour mixture. Beat at low speed until blended after each addition. Stir in vanilla. Spoon half of batter into a greased 13"x9" baking pan. Spread reserved cranberry mixture over batter. Drop remaining batter by rounded tablespoonfuls over cranberry mixture. Sprinkle with ginger topping.

Bake at 350 degrees for 32 to 35 minutes or until a toothpick inserted in center comes out clean. Cool in pan on a wire rack. Serves 12.

Cookies 'n' Cream Cake

18½-oz. pkg. white cake mix
1¼ c. water
⅓ c. oil
1 t. vanilla extract

3 eggs
1 c. chocolate sandwich cookies, crushed

Combine cake mix, water, oil, vanilla and eggs in a large mixing bowl; blend at low speed with an electric mixer until just moistened. Blend at high speed 2 minutes; gently fold in crushed cookies. Line 2 8" round cake pans with wax paper; grease and flour pans. Pour batter into pans; bake at 350 degrees for 25 minutes or until a toothpick inserted in center comes out clean. Cool 10 minutes; remove from pans to a wire rack to cool completely. Spread with Frosting. Serves 12.

Frosting:

½ c. butter or shortening
1 t. vanilla extract

4 c. powdered sugar
¼ c. milk

Beat together butter and vanilla until creamy. Add powdered sugar and milk alternately to creamed mixture, beating until desired consistency.

Shari Miller
Hobart, IN

For even more chocolatey taste, try using chocolate sandwich cookies with chocolate filling...yum!

Shari

Peppermint Candy Cheesecake

1 c. graham cracker crumbs
¾ c. sugar, divided
6 T. butter, melted and divided
1½ c. sour cream
2 eggs
1 T. all-purpose flour
2 t. vanilla extract

2 (8-oz. pkgs.) cream cheese, softened
¼ c. peppermint candies, coarsely crushed
Optional: frozen whipped topping, thawed; crushed peppermint candies

Drizzle strawberry syrup on each slice right before serving for a merry little touch.

Bobbi

Blend crumbs, ¼ cup sugar and ¼ cup melted butter in bottom of an ungreased 8" round springform pan; press evenly over bottom. Blend sour cream, remaining sugar, eggs, flour and vanilla in a blender or food processor until smooth, stopping to scrape sides. Add cream cheese and blend; stir in remaining 2 tablespoons melted butter until completely smooth. Fold in crushed candies and pour over crust. Bake at 325 degrees for 45 minutes. Remove from oven and run a knife around edge of pan. Cool, then refrigerate overnight. Loosen pan sides and remove springform; serve garnished with whipped topping and crushed candies, if desired. Serves 12.

Bobbi Carney
Hobart, IN

Chocolate-Cappuccino Cheesecake

This makes an absolutely delicious cheesecake.

Sandy

1½ c. pecans, finely chopped
1½ c. chocolate wafer cookies, crushed
⅓ c. butter, melted
2 c. chocolate chips, melted and divided
2 (8-oz.) pkgs. cream cheese, softened

1 c. brown sugar, packed
4 eggs
1 c. sour cream
⅓ c. cold coffee
2 t. vanilla extract
½ c. chocolate chips
⅓ c. whipping cream
2 T. powdered sugar

Combine pecans, cookies and butter; press into the bottom of a greased 9" springform pan. Bake at 350 degrees for 8 minutes; cool in pan 10 minutes. Drizzle crust with ½ cup melted chocolate; chill 40 minutes.

Beat cream cheese with an electric mixer until creamy. Gradually add brown sugar, beating well. Add eggs, one at a time, beating after each addition. Add remaining 1½ cups melted chocolate, sour cream, coffee and vanilla; beat until smooth. Pour into pan; bake at 325 degrees for one hour and 5 minutes (center will not be completely set). Turn oven off and partially open oven door; leave cake in oven one hour. Cool completely. Cover and chill 8 hours.

Remove sides of pan. Heat ½ cup chocolate chips and whipping cream over low heat, stirring constantly. Stir in powdered sugar until smooth. Drizzle topping over cake. Serves 12.

Sandy Stacy
Medway, OH

Mini Cheesecakes

These look so pretty on your dessert table.

3 (8-oz.) pkgs. cream cheese,
   softened
1½ c. sugar, divided
5 eggs

1½ t. vanilla extract
1 c. sour cream
2 (21-oz.) cans cherry pie filling

   Beat together cream cheese and one cup sugar. Add eggs, one at a time, beating well after each addition. Add vanilla and mix again.

   Pour batter into paper-lined mini muffin cups, filling ¾ full. Bake at 350 degrees for 20 minutes. Remove from oven; let stand 5 minutes. Combine sour cream and remaining ½ cup sugar. Top each cheesecake with ½ teaspoon of the sour cream mixture and return to the oven for 5 minutes. When cooled, top each cheesecake with one cherry and a little of the filling. Keep refrigerated. Makes 8 dozen.

Perfect Pecan Pie

3 eggs
½ c. sugar
¼ t. salt
3 T. butter, melted
1 c. dark corn syrup

1 t. vanilla extract
9-inch pie crust
2 c. pecan halves
Optional: vanilla ice cream

Whisk together eggs and next 5 ingredients until thoroughly blended. Stir in pecans. Fit pie crust into a 9" pie plate according to package directions. Fold edges under and crimp. Pour filling into pie crust.

Bake at 350 degrees on lower rack 40 minutes or until pie is set, covering edges with aluminum foil after 15 minutes. Cool completely on a wire rack. Serve with vanilla ice cream, if desired. Serves 6.

sweet offering

For an oh-so-pretty gift, top pies with an inverted pie plate and secure both together with a bandanna.

Chocolate Marshmallow Pie

16 marshmallows
4 (1.45-oz.) milk chocolate
  candy bars with almonds

½ c. milk
8-oz. carton whipping cream
9-inch graham cracker crust

Heat marshmallows, candy bars and milk in a double boiler until marshmallows and chocolate melt; stir often. Remove from heat; stir in whipping cream. Pour into pie crust; refrigerate until firm. Serves 8.

Brenda Neal
Taneyville, MO

New England Pumpkin Pie

Make this special pie for your gathering.

6 T. brown sugar, packed
2 T. sugar
2 t. cinnamon
½ t. nutmeg
½ t. salt
¼ t. ground cloves

½ c. molasses
3 eggs, separated
15-oz. can pumpkin
1½ c. half-and-half
2 T. rum or 1 t. rum extract
2 (9-inch) pie crusts

Combine first 6 ingredients. Add molasses and egg yolks; mix well. Stir in pumpkin, half-and-half and rum. Beat egg whites until stiff; fold into pumpkin mixture. Pour into unbaked pie crusts. Bake at 425 degrees for 30 minutes or until knife inserted in center comes out clean. Makes 2 pies.

Joan Merling
Bethel, CT

Christmas

Bar Harbor Cranberry Pie

2 c. cranberries
1½ c. sugar, divided
½ c. chopped pecans
2 eggs, beaten
1 c. all-purpose flour

½ c. butter, melted
¼ c. shortening, melted
Optional: whipped cream,
    cinnamon

Lightly butter a 9" glass pie plate; spread cranberries over bottom. Sprinkle evenly with ½ cup sugar and pecans; set aside. In a separate bowl, add eggs and remaining one cup sugar; mix well. Blend in flour, butter and shortening; beat well after each addition. Pour over cranberries; bake at 325 degrees for 55 to 60 minutes. Garnish each serving with a dollop of whipped cream and a sprinkle of cinnamon, if desired. Serves 8.

Jean Hayes
La Porte, TX

Frozen berries can also be used... no need to thaw before preparing this pretty pie.

Jean

Mocha Pecan Mud Pie

Two store-bought ice creams pack lots of flavor into this frozen dessert.

12 chocolate sandwich cookies, crumbled

3 T. butter or margarine, melted

1 egg white, lightly beaten

1¼ c. chopped pecans

¼ c. sugar

1 pt. coffee ice cream, softened

1 pt. chocolate ice cream, softened

12 chocolate sandwich cookies, coarsely chopped and divided

Optional: frozen whipped topping, thawed, additional cookies and pecans, coarsely chopped

Stir together cookie crumbs and butter. Press into a 9" pie plate. Brush with egg white.

Bake at 350 degrees for 5 minutes. Cool on a wire rack.

Place pecans on a lightly greased baking sheet; sprinkle with sugar. Bake at 350 degrees for 8 to 10 minutes. Cool.

Stir together ice creams, one cup coarsely chopped cookies and one cup pecans; spoon into crust. Freeze 10 minutes. Press remaining coarsely chopped cookies and pecans on top. Cover and freeze at least 8 hours. Garnish with whipped topping and additional chopped cookies and pecans, if desired. Serves 8.

pies galore

Consider having a Pie Night. Invite family & friends to bring their favorite pie to share. And don't forget copies of the recipes…someone's sure to ask!

Mile-High Frozen Strawberry Pie

11¾-oz. jar hot fudge topping, divided
9-inch graham cracker crust
1 pt. strawberry ice cream, slightly softened

5 c. vanilla ice cream
1 pt. fresh strawberries, hulled and sliced

Spread ¼ cup fudge topping over bottom of crust. Spoon strawberry ice cream evenly into crust. Freeze until firm. Mound tiny scoops of vanilla ice cream over strawberry ice cream. Gently place strawberry slices between ice cream scoops. Cover and freeze pie at least one hour or until firm. Place remaining fudge topping in a small saucepan. Cook over medium-low heat until thoroughly heated. Let pie stand at room temperature 5 minutes before serving; slice pie into wedges. Spoon fudge topping over each serving. Makes one pie.

Peanut Butter-Ice Cream Pie

6 (.8-oz.) peanut butter cup candies, frozen and chopped
1 qt. vanilla ice cream, slightly softened

9-inch chocolate cookie crust
20 caramels, unwrapped
⅔ c. evaporated milk
3 T. creamy peanut butter

Combine chopped peanut butter cup candies and vanilla ice cream in a large bowl; freeze until ice cream is almost firm. Spoon ice cream into chocolate cookie crust, mounding up in center. Cover and freeze until firm. Combine caramels and evaporated milk in a medium saucepan. Cook over medium-low heat, stirring constantly, until mixture is smooth. Remove caramel sauce from heat and stir in peanut butter. Spoon warm sauce over each serving. Makes one pie.

Caramel Apple Crisp

½ c. plus ⅓ c. all-purpose flour,
   divided
1 c. sugar, divided
½ t. cinnamon
¼ t. nutmeg
40 caramels, unwrapped and
   quartered
9 c. Granny Smith or
   other cooking apples, peeled,
   cored and sliced

¼ c. orange juice
¼ c. butter, cut into pieces
⅔ c. quick-cooking oats,
   uncooked
½ c. chopped walnuts

Combine ½ cup flour, ½ cup sugar, cinnamon and nutmeg in a large bowl; add caramels and stir to coat.

Toss sliced apples with orange juice in another bowl; add to caramel mixture and combine well. Spoon apple mixture into a lightly greased 13"x9" baking pan.

Combine remaining ½ cup sugar and remaining ⅓ cup flour in a small bowl; cut in butter with a pastry blender or 2 knives until mixture is crumbly. Stir in oats and walnuts; sprinkle topping mixture over apples. Bake at 350 degrees for one hour or until apples are tender. Serves 15 to 20.

Jo Ann
Gooseberry Patch

Let your kids help unwrap caramels for this fruit dessert.

Jo Ann

Bread Pudding

Day-old bread is best for soaking up the liquid in this oh-so-decadent dessert.

4 eggs

1½ c. sugar

3 (12-oz.) cans evaporated milk

½ c. butter, melted

1 T. vanilla extract

2 t. cinnamon

6 c. French bread, torn into
pieces and packed

1 Granny Smith apple, peeled,
cored and chopped

1½ c. walnuts, coarsely chopped
and toasted

1 c. golden raisins

Whisk eggs in a large bowl. Whisk in sugar and next 4 ingredients. Fold in bread and next 3 ingredients, stirring until bread is moistened. Pour into a greased 13"x9" baking pan.

Bake, uncovered, at 350 degrees for 50 minutes or until set. Cut into squares. Serve warm with Rum Sauce. Serves 12.

Rum Sauce:

2 (14-oz.) cans sweetened
condensed milk

2 T. dark rum or 1 t. rum extract

1 T. vanilla extract

Pour condensed milk into a small saucepan; cook over medium heat until hot, stirring often. Remove from heat; stir in rum and vanilla. Serve warm. Makes 2½ cups.

Mom Ford's Chocolate Chip Cookies

½ c. shortening

⅓ c. sugar

⅓ c. brown sugar, packed

1 egg

½ t. vanilla extract

1 c. all-purpose flour

½ t. baking soda

¼ t. salt

1 c. semi-sweet chocolate chips

½ c. chopped pecans

Beat shortening at medium speed with an electric mixer until fluffy. Gradually add sugars, beating mixture well. Add egg and vanilla, beating until blended.

Stir together flour, baking soda and salt; add to shortening mixture, mixing well. Stir in chocolate chips and pecans.

Drop dough by tablespoonfuls onto ungreased baking sheets. Bake at 350 degrees for 10 to 12 minutes. Transfer to wire racks to cool. Makes 2 dozen.

Marshmallow Cookie Spiders

Spooky but sweet, these spiders are easy to fix for school parties.

black licorice rope for legs

4¼-oz. tube white icing

9-oz. pkg. chocolate-covered
    marshmallow cookies

assorted candies for eyes

For each spider, cut 4 pieces of licorice measuring from 2" to 3" in length. Using a knife, cut each licorice piece in half lengthwise. Place each pair of legs opposite each other, flat side down, on lightly greased wax paper. Cover inside ends of licorice with icing. Gently press cookie onto icing and legs. Use icing to "glue" the candies onto cookie for eyes. Allow icing to set up and carefully transfer cookie spiders to serving plates. Makes 8.

Vanilla-Dipped Gingersnaps

2½ c. sugar, divided
1½ c. oil
2 eggs
½ c. molasses
4 c. all-purpose flour
4 t. baking soda

1 T. ground ginger
2 t. cinnamon
1 t. salt
2 (11-oz.) pkgs. white chocolate chips
¼ c. shortening

Combine 2 cups sugar and oil in a mixing bowl; mix well. Add eggs, one at a time, beating well after each addition. Stir in molasses.

Combine flour, baking soda, ginger, cinnamon and salt in a separate bowl; gradually blend into molasses mixture. Shape dough into one-inch balls and roll in remaining sugar; place 2 inches apart on ungreased baking sheets. Bake at 350 degrees for 15 to 20 minutes or until cookie springs back when lightly touched. Remove to wire racks to cool.

Melt white chocolate chips and shortening together in a small saucepan over low heat, stirring until smooth. Dip each cookie halfway into mixture; allow excess to drip off. Place cookies on wax paper to harden. Makes about 7 dozen.

Krista Starnes
Beaufort, SC

This is a cookie recipe I make every Christmas for friends & family. These are not only pretty, but they taste delicious.

Krista

lunch-box surprise

Surprise 'em at lunch by slipping cookies inside vellum envelopes and tying them closed with shoestring licorice!

Christmas

Sugar Cookies

2 (18-oz.) pkgs. refrigerated
   sugar cookie dough

Optional: drinking straw
assorted candies and sprinkles

Roll out dough to ¼-inch thickness. Cut out with cookie cutters (for cookie ornaments, before baking, use the straw to make a hole in each cookie for hanging). Place on ungreased baking sheets and bake at 350 degrees for 5 to 7 minutes or until golden. Decorate with Sugar Cookie Frosting, candies and sprinkles. Makes 36 to 40.

Sugar Cookie Frosting:

5 c. powdered sugar
5½ to 6½ T. water

1½ t. almond extract
paste food coloring

Combine powdered sugar, water and almond extract in a medium bowl; beat until smooth. Transfer frosting into small bowls and tint with food coloring. Spread onto cooled cookies.

storage containers

Search flea markets, yard sales or antique shops for unique biscuit or pickle jars and old-style bottles. They're just right to fill with sweet treats for friends or to set on your counter filled with after-school snacks!

Yummy Cappuccino Bites

⅓ c. butter, softened

1 c. brown sugar, packed

⅔ c. baking cocoa

1 T. instant coffee granules

1 t. baking soda

1 t. cinnamon

2 egg whites

⅓ c. vanilla yogurt

1½ c. all-purpose flour

⅓ c. sugar

Combine butter and brown sugar. Stir in cocoa, coffee granules, baking soda and cinnamon. Mix in egg whites and yogurt; blend in flour. Place sugar in a small bowl; drop dough by heaping teaspoonfuls into sugar. Roll into one-inch balls and place 2 inches apart on ungreased baking sheets. Bake at 350 degrees for 8 to 10 minutes; cool on wire racks. Makes about 2½ dozen.

Macaroon Tartlets

1 c. butter, softened

1 c. sugar, divided

3 eggs, divided

1 t. vanilla extract

2 c. all-purpose flour

1 lb. almond paste

½ t. almond extract

½ c. slivered almonds

Beat butter at medium speed with an electric mixer until creamy; gradually add ½ cup sugar, beating well. Add one egg and vanilla; beat well. Gradually add flour; beat well.

Shape dough into 48 (one-inch) balls; press balls into lightly greased mini muffin cups, pressing evenly into bottom and up sides. Set aside. Beat almond paste at medium speed until creamy; gradually add remaining ½ cup sugar, beating well. Add almond extract and remaining 2 eggs, beating well. Spoon mixture into prepared shells. Top each tartlet with 3 slivered almonds. Bake at 325 degrees for 25 minutes or until golden. Cool in pans on wire racks 10 minutes; remove to wire racks and cool completely. Makes 4 dozen.

Chocolate-Caramel Thumbprints

A gooey caramel center guarantees these cookies will disappear quickly!

½ c. butter or margarine, softened

½ c. sugar

2 (1-oz.) sqs. semi-sweet baking chocolate, melted

1 egg yolk

2 t. vanilla extract

1¼ c. all-purpose flour

1 t. baking soda

¼ t. salt

¾ c. pecans, very finely chopped

16 caramels, unwrapped

2½ T. whipping cream

⅔ c. semi-sweet chocolate chips

2 t. shortening

Beat butter at medium speed with an electric mixer until creamy; gradually add sugar, beating well. Add melted chocolate and egg yolk, beating until blended. Stir in vanilla. Combine flour, soda and salt; add to butter mixture, beating well. Cover and chill one hour.

Shape dough into one-inch balls; roll balls in chopped pecans. Place balls one inch apart on greased baking sheets. Press thumb gently into center of each ball, leaving a thumbprint.

Bake at 350 degrees for 12 minutes or until set. Meanwhile, combine caramels and whipping cream in top of a double boiler over simmering water. Cook over medium-low heat, stirring constantly, until caramels melt and mixture is smooth.

Remove cookies from oven; cool slightly and press center of each cookie again. Quickly spoon ¾ teaspoon caramel mixture into center of each cookie. Remove cookies to wire racks to cool.

Place chocolate chips and shortening in a heavy-duty plastic zipping bag; seal bag. Microwave on high one to 1½ minutes; squeeze bag until chocolate melts. Snip a tiny hole in one corner of bag, using scissors. Drizzle chocolate over cooled cookies. Makes about 2½ dozen.

Pumpkin Spice Bars

18¼-oz. pkg. spice cake mix
½ c. plus 1 T. butter, melted and
  divided
½ c. pecans, finely chopped
1 T. plus 1 t. vanilla extract,
  divided
8-oz. pkg. cream cheese,
  softened
⅓ c. light brown sugar, packed
1 c. canned pumpkin
1 egg
½ c. white chocolate, finely
  chopped
⅓ c. long-cooking oats,
  uncooked
Optional: powdered sugar

Combine cake mix, ½ cup melted butter, pecans and one table-spoon vanilla, mixing well with a fork. Reserve one cup crumbs for streusel topping. Press remaining crumbs into a lightly greased 13"x9" baking pan.

Bake at 350 degrees for 13 to 15 minutes or until puffy and set. Cool in pan on a wire rack 20 minutes.

Beat cream cheese at medium speed with an electric mixer 30 seconds or until creamy. Add brown sugar, pumpkin, egg and remaining one teaspoon vanilla; beat until blended. Pour filling over baked crust.

Stir white chocolate, remaining one tablespoon melted butter and oats into reserved one cup streusel. Sprinkle over filling.

Bake at 350 degrees for 30 minutes or until edges begin to brown and center is set. Cool completely in pan on a wire rack. Sprinkle with powdered sugar, if desired. Cut into bars. Serve at room temperature or chilled. Makes 2 dozen.

Lemon-Coconut Bars

2 c. all-purpose flour
1 c. powdered sugar, divided
1 c. butter, softened

½ c. slivered almonds, chopped
  and toasted
1 c. sweetened flaked coconut

Combine flour and ½ cup powdered sugar. Cut butter into flour mixture with a pastry blender until crumbly; stir in almonds. Firmly press mixture into a lightly greased 13"x9" baking pan.

Bake at 350 degrees for 20 to 25 minutes or until light golden.

Stir together Lemon Chess Pie Filling and coconut; pour over baked crust.

Bake at 350 degrees for 30 to 35 minutes or until set. Cool in pan on a wire rack. Sprinkle with remaining ½ cup powdered sugar; cut into bars. Makes 32.

Lemon Chess Pie Filling:

2 c. sugar
4 eggs
¼ c. butter, melted
¼ c. milk
1 T. lemon zest

¼ c. lemon juice
1 T. all-purpose flour
1 T. cornmeal
¼ t. salt

Whisk together all ingredients. Use filling immediately. Makes about 3 cups.

Raspberry Bars

1 c. butter, softened
¾ c. sugar
1 egg
½ t. vanilla extract

2½ c. all-purpose flour
10-oz. jar seedless raspberry jam
½ c. chopped pecans, toasted

Beat butter and sugar until creamy. Add egg and vanilla, beating until blended. Add flour, beating until blended. Reserving one cup dough, press remaining dough firmly into a lightly greased 9"x9" baking pan. Spread jam evenly over crust. Stir pecans into reserved dough. Sprinkle evenly over jam layer. Bake at 350 degrees for 25 to 28 minutes or until golden. Cool completely on a wire rack. Makes about 1½ dozen.

Vickie
Gooseberry Patch

Whip up these fruity treats for a potluck and watch them disappear!

Vickie

shipping cookies

Place pieces of wax paper between cookie layers and add mini marshmallows to make sure cookies don't move around. Tuck in a couple of packages of cocoa for a great gift!

Buckeye
Brownies

Buckeye Brownies

19½-oz. pkg. brownie mix
2 c. powdered sugar
½ c. plus 6 T. butter, softened
   and divided

1 c. creamy peanut butter
6-oz. pkg. semi-sweet chocolate
   chips

Prepare and bake brownie mix in a greased 13"x9" baking pan according to package directions. Let cool.

Mix together powdered sugar, ½ cup butter and peanut butter; spread over cooled brownies. Chill one hour.

Melt together chocolate chips and remaining 6 tablespoons butter in a saucepan over low heat, stirring occasionally. Spread over brownies. Let cool; cut into squares. Makes 2 to 3 dozen.

Heather Prentice
Mars, PA

Chocolate and peanut butter... tastes just like buckeye candies.

Heather

Vickie's Chocolate Fondue

Delicious dipping for squares of pound cake, mandarin oranges, cherries and strawberries!

24-oz. pkg. semi-sweet
   chocolate chips
1 pt. whipping cream

6 T. corn syrup
6 T. orange extract

Melt chocolate chips in the top of a double boiler; add remaining ingredients and stir to blend. When fondue is warm, spoon into a fondue pot or small slow cooker on low heat to keep sauce warm. Makes 2½ cups.

Vickie
Gooseberry Patch

Pucker Pops

1 pt. lime sherbet
1¾ c. water
3 oz. frozen limeade
    concentrate

24 wooden craft sticks

Combine first 3 ingredients in container of an electric blender; process until smooth. Pour mixture into ice cube trays; freeze 30 minutes or until almost firm. Insert a wooden stick into center of each cube; freeze until firm. Remove from trays and wrap in heavy-duty plastic wrap. Store in freezer. Makes 2 dozen.

Speedy Sorbet

What a fun way to eat fruit! For pineapple sorbet, substitute 2 (20-ounce) cans chunk pineapple in heavy syrup for pie filling. For strawberry sorbet, substitute 3 (10-ounce) packages frozen strawberries in syrup for pie filling.

2 (21-oz.) cans blueberry or
    cherry pie filling

Freeze unopened cans of pie filling until frozen solid, at least 18 hours or up to one month. Submerge unopened cans in hot water one to 2 minutes. Open both ends of cans and slide frozen mixture into a bowl. Break into chunks. Position knife blade in food processor bowl; add chunks. Process until smooth, stopping as necessary to scrape down sides. Pour fruit mixture into an 8"x8" baking pan. Freeze until firm. Let stand 10 minutes before serving. Serves 6.

4th of July

Watermelon Fruitsicles

5-lb. watermelon wedge, seeded
   and cubed
½ c. sugar

1 env. unflavored gelatin
1 T. lemon juice

Place half of watermelon in container of an electric blender; process until smooth. Repeat procedure with remaining watermelon. Strain watermelon purée into a large measuring cup, discarding pulp. Reserve 4 cups watermelon juice.

Combine one cup juice and sugar in a saucepan. Sprinkle gelatin over mixture; let stand one minute. Cook over medium heat, stirring constantly, until sugar and gelatin dissolve. Add gelatin mixture to remaining 3 cups watermelon juice; stir in lemon juice and let cool. Pour into ⅓-cup frozen pop molds; freeze. Makes one dozen.

Pumpkin Pie Ice Cream Fantasy

Two holiday dessert classics are swirled with caramel and pecans... what's not to love¿

1 baked pumpkin pie
½ gal. vanilla ice cream

caramel topping
pecan halves, toasted

Place pie in freezer one hour; remove pie from freezer and chop ¾ of pie into one-inch pieces. Allow ice cream to stand 8 to 10 minutes to slightly soften. Spoon ice cream into a large bowl. Gently fold in pie pieces until blended.

To serve, scoop each serving into a wine glass or dessert bowl. Drizzle with caramel topping and top with pecans. Serves 12.

Ultimate Fudge Sauce, page 272

giftable goodies

There's always a reason for giving throughout the year, and the best gifts come from the heart, or in our case…the kitchen! Give neighborhood friends a jar of Festive Cranberry Honey (page 271) at Christmastime, pass out goodie bags of Caramel-Pecan Popcorn Crunch (page 299) to trick-or-treaters on Halloween night and surprise Dad with White Chocolate Cookies 'n' Cream Fudge (page 303) on Fathers' Day. Show your loved ones how much you care throughout the year with any of the yummy homemade gifts found in this chapter.

Go-Team Chili Seasoning

2 T. dried, minced onion

1 T. all-purpose flour

1½ t. chili powder

1 t. salt

1 t. sugar

½ t. garlic powder

½ t. cayenne pepper

½ t. ground cumin

Combine all ingredients; store in an airtight container. Attach instructions. Makes ¼ cup.

Instructions:

Brown one pound ground beef in a skillet; drain. Return beef to skillet and add seasoning mix, 2 (15½-ounce) cans kidney beans and 2 (16-ounce) cans stewed tomatoes. Bring to a boil; reduce heat and simmer 10 minutes, stirring occasionally. Serves 4 to 6.

Olive Pesto

¾ c. pitted Kalamata or ripe
    olives
½ c. fresh flat-leaf parsley sprigs,
    packed
¼ c. fresh basil leaves, packed

1 shallot, chopped
2 cloves garlic, pressed
3 T. extra-virgin olive oil
¼ c. grated Parmesan cheese

Process first 5 ingredients in a blender until minced, stopping to scrape down sides. Add oil and cheese; process until blended. Transfer to a small bowl. Cover and chill, if desired. Store in refrigerator. Makes one cup.

Sun-Dried Tomato & Roasted Garlic Pesto

1 bulb garlic, unpeeled
3 T. extra-virgin olive oil,
    divided
8½-oz. jar sun-dried tomatoes,
    packed in olive oil

⅓ c. fresh flat-leaf parsley sprigs,
    packed
2 T. green onions, chopped
2 T. grated Parmesan cheese

Cut off pointed end of garlic; place garlic on a piece of aluminum foil and drizzle with 2 tablespoons oil. Fold foil to seal. Bake at 350 degrees for 40 minutes; cool 10 minutes. Squeeze pulp from garlic cloves and mash with a fork. Place roasted garlic, sun-dried tomatoes, parsley and green onions in a blender or food processor; process until finely minced. Add remaining one tablespoon oil and cheese; process until blended. Transfer to a small bowl; cover and chill. Makes 1¼ cups.

Festive Cranberry
Honey

Christmas

Festive Cranberry Honey

This recipe makes enough to give several gifts.

3 (16-oz.) cans whole-berry
    cranberry sauce

12-oz. jar orange marmalade
1½ c. honey

    Place cranberry sauce and marmalade in a large microwave-safe bowl. Microwave on high 2 minutes or until melted. Stir in honey until well blended. Spoon into jars with lids. Store in the refrigerator. Serve with breads or use as a glaze for meat. Makes about 8 cups.

Fathers' Day

Homemade Maple Syrup

4 c. sugar
2 T. corn syrup
½ c. brown sugar, packed

2 c. water
1 t. vanilla extract
1 t. maple flavoring

    Stir together first 4 ingredients in a saucepan until sugar dissolves. Heat over medium heat until boiling; boil one to 2 minutes. Remove from heat and cool 5 to 10 minutes. Stir in vanilla and maple flavoring. Makes about 4 cups.

Jana Warnell
Kalispell, MT

I always keep a batch in my fridge...it's yummy!

Jana

Ultimate Fudge Sauce

(pictured on page 266)

This sauce is rich, thick and so delicious!

Vickie

1 c. heavy whipping cream
¾ c. sugar
8 oz. unsweetened chocolate, finely chopped

⅓ c. corn syrup
¼ c. unsalted butter
1½ t. vanilla extract
⅛ t. salt

Combine whipping cream and sugar in a heavy saucepan. Place over medium heat and cook, stirring constantly, until sugar dissolves. Stir in chocolate, corn syrup and butter. Cook over medium-low heat, stirring occasionally, until chocolate melts and all ingredients are blended. Remove from heat; stir in vanilla and salt. Let cool to room temperature. Transfer sauce to jars with tight-fitting lids. Store in refrigerator. To serve, spoon sauce into a microwave-safe bowl and microwave on high in 20-second intervals until pourable. Makes 2½ cups.

Vickie
Gooseberry Patch

Apple Pie in a Jar

Pour in a pie crust and bake for a yummy homemade apple pie.

5 to 6 lbs. apples, peeled, cored
   and sliced
4½ c. sugar
1 c. cornstarch
2 t. cinnamon
¼ t. nutmeg

1 t. salt
10 c. water
3 T. lemon juice
7 (1-qt.) canning jars and lids,
   sterilized

Pack apples tightly in jars. In a large saucepan, cook sugar, cornstarch, cinnamon, nutmeg, salt and water over medium-high heat until thick and bubbly; add lemon juice. Cover apples with syrup, leaving ½ inch headspace. Wipe rims and secure lids and rings. Process in a boiling-water bath for 20 minutes. Set jars on a towel to cool. Check for seals. Makes 7 jars.

Beth Landis
Mentone, IN

Toffee Peanuts

Use this recipe method to candy-coat any mix of nuts, such as blanched almonds, whole cashews, walnut halves or a combination of the three.

1½ c. sugar
¼ c. butter
½ c. water

4 c. raw peanuts, shelled
½ t. salt
¼ t. cinnamon

Lightly grease a large jelly-roll pan; set aside.

Stir together sugar, butter and ½ cup water in a large deep skillet over medium heat; cook, stirring constantly, 3 minutes or until butter melts and sugar dissolves.

Increase heat to medium-high; add peanuts and cook, stirring often, 15 minutes or until mixture becomes dry. Reduce heat to medium; continue to cook, stirring often, 6 to 9 minutes or until sugar melts, is golden and coats nuts. (Do not stir constantly.) Sprinkle with salt and cinnamon; stir well. Spread nuts in a single layer on prepared pan. Cool completely; break nuts apart. Store in an airtight container up to 2 weeks. Makes 7 cups.

good neighbor surprise

Make a cone shape from pretty scrapbook paper. Glue in place. Punch a hole in each side of the cone and slide ribbon or rick rack through to make a handle; tie each end to secure. Place a bag filled with your favorite goodies in the cone. Slipped over a doorknob, it's sure to be a welcome Good Neighbor Day surprise!

New Year's

Spicy Vanilla Pecans

When you give these pecans as gifts...be prepared to share the recipe, too!

1 lb. pecan halves	¼ t. salt
6 c. water	¼ t. cinnamon
½ c. sugar	¼ t. nutmeg
3 T. butter, melted	¼ t. allspice
1 T. corn syrup	⅛ t. pepper
1 T. vanilla extract	

Boil pecans in water in a saucepan one minute; drain. Immediately toss pecans in a large bowl with sugar, butter, corn syrup and vanilla; mix well. Cover bowl and let sit 12 to 24 hours.

Place pecans on an ungreased 15"x10" jelly-roll pan. Bake at 325 degrees for 30 minutes, stirring every 5 minutes. While pecans are baking, combine remaining ingredients in a large bowl. After baking pecans, immediately toss them with spices until well coated. Spread pecans in a single layer on jelly-roll pan and let cool. Makes 5½ cups.

Dipped & Drizzled Pretzels

A pretty and tasty gift!

18 oz. white melting chocolate, divided

4 c. small pretzel twists
pink paste food coloring

Melt 12 ounces white chocolate in a double boiler. Dip pretzels in melted chocolate and place on wax paper to harden. Melt remaining 6 ounces white chocolate in a small saucepan and tint pink; drizzle over pretzels. Allow to harden. Store in an airtight container. Makes 5 cups.

Jo Ann's Walnut-Oatmeal Cookie Mix

2¼ c. quick-cooking oats, uncooked
1½ c. all-purpose flour
1 c. chopped walnuts
¾ c. brown sugar, packed

½ c. sugar
½ c. chocolate chips
1¼ t. cinnamon
¾ t. baking soda
¼ t. nutmeg

Combine all ingredients; place in a decorated box. Attach instructions.

Instructions:

Place mix in a large bowl. Stir in one cup softened butter, one egg and one teaspoon vanilla extract. Drop by tablespoonfuls onto ungreased baking sheets. Bake at 350 degrees for 10 minutes; cool. Makes 3 dozen.

Jo Ann
Gooseberry Patch

By giving most of the ingredients for these cookies in a decorated box, fresh-baked cookies will be ready in a snap.

Jo Ann

Big Crunchy Sugar Cookies

These goodies earned their name from a coating of coarse sugar.

1 c. butter, softened
1 c. sugar
1 egg
1½ t. vanilla extract

2 c. all-purpose flour
½ t. baking powder
¼ t. salt
assorted coarse decorator sugars

Beat butter at medium speed with an electric mixer until creamy. Gradually add sugar, beating until smooth. Add egg and vanilla, beating until blended.

Combine flour, baking powder and salt; gradually add to butter mixture, beating just until blended. Shape dough into a ball; cover and chill 2 hours.

Divide dough into 3 portions. Work with one portion at a time, storing remaining dough in refrigerator. Shape dough into 1½-inch balls; roll each ball in decorator sugar. Place 2 inches apart on parchment paper-lined baking sheets. Gently press and flatten each ball of dough to ¾-inch thickness. Bake at 375 degrees for 13 to 15 minutes or until edges of cookies are lightly golden. Cool 5 minutes on baking sheets; remove to wire racks to cool. Makes 1½ dozen.

Aunt Neal's Old-Fashioned Tea Cakes

This southern Georgia version of tea cakes dates back to the turn of the twentieth century!

These delicious tea cakes were made by my Aunt Cornelia ("Neal") on special occasions and holidays, using homemade hand-churned butter and eggs she gathered from the henhouse.

Ana

1 c. butter, softened
1 c. sugar
1 egg, lightly beaten
1 t. vanilla extract
3 c. all-purpose flour

1 t. baking powder
½ t. baking soda
½ t. salt
½ c. milk
sparkling white sugar

Beat butter at medium speed with an electric mixer until creamy; gradually add one cup sugar, beating well. Add egg and vanilla; beat well.

Combine flour and next 3 ingredients; add to butter mixture alternately with milk, beginning and ending with flour mixture. Mix at low speed after each addition just until blended. Shape dough into 2 discs. Wrap in wax paper and chill at least one hour.

Roll each disc to ¼-inch thickness on a floured surface. Cut with a 3½-inch round cutter; place one inch apart on lightly greased baking sheets. Sprinkle with sparkling sugar. Bake at 400 degrees for 7 to 8 minutes or until edges are lightly golden. Cool one minute on baking sheets; remove to wire racks to cool. Makes 2 dozen.

Ana Kelly
Birmingham, AL

Christmas

Mom's Gingerbread Cookies

½ c. shortening
2½ c. all-purpose flour, divided
½ c. sugar
½ c. molasses
1 egg

1 t. baking soda
1 t. ground ginger
½ t. cinnamon
½ t. ground cloves
candy-coated chocolates

Beat shortening until softened. Add about 1¼ cups flour and next 7 ingredients. Beat until thoroughly combined. Stir in remaining 1¼ cups flour. Divide dough in half. Cover dough and chill 3 hours or until easily handled. Roll each half of the dough to ⅛" to ¼" thickness. Cut with a 4½-inch gingerbread man cookie cutter. Place on ungreased baking sheets and bake at 375 degrees for 7 to 8 minutes or until edges are firm. Decorate with Powdered Sugar Frosting and candies. Makes 2 dozen.

Powdered Sugar Frosting:

1 c. powdered sugar
¼ t. vanilla extract

1 T. milk

Combine all ingredients, stirring until smooth. Transfer frosting to a pastry bag fitted with a small round tip. Pipe frosting onto cookies. Makes ⅓ cup.

Michele Urdahl
Litchfield, MN

When I was little, Mom and I used to bake gingerbread men together at Christmastime. I remember peeking through the oven door, waiting for one of them to get up off the pan, just like in the story!

Michele

Brownie Buttons

16-oz. pkg. refrigerated
   mini brownie bites
   dough

11-oz. bag assorted mini peanut
   butter cup candies and
   chocolate-coated caramels

Spray mini muffin cups with non-stick vegetable spray. Spoon brownie dough evenly into each cup, filling almost full. Bake at 350 degrees for 19 to 20 minutes. Cool in pans 3 to 4 minutes; gently press a candy into each baked brownie until top of candy is level with top of brownie. Cool 10 minutes in pans. Gently twist each brownie to remove from pan. Cool on a wire rack. Makes 20.

box of love

Tell a best friend no one else can fill her shoes! Cover the lid of a plain shoe box with pictures of shoes cut from magazines or catalogs. Fill the box with homemade treats and wrap the box with pretty cotton string.

Peppermint Pinwheels

½ c. shortening
½ c. butter, softened
1¼ c. sugar, divided
1 egg
1½ t. almond extract
1 t. vanilla extract
2½ c. all-purpose flour

1 t. salt
½ t. red food coloring
2 t. meringue powder
¼ c. water
¼ c. peppermint sticks, crushed, or coarse sanding sugar

Mix together shortening, butter, one cup sugar, egg, almond and vanilla extracts. Sift together flour and salt; blend into butter mixture. Divide dough in half and blend red food coloring into one half.

Chill both halves until firm. Roll light dough on a lightly floured surface to form a 6"x6" square. Roll red half to same size and lay on top of light dough. Wrap in plastic wrap and chill until firm. Roll the double layer with a rolling pin to a 12"x12" square. Tightly roll up jelly-roll style; wrap in plastic wrap and chill one hour.

Slice chilled dough into ¼-inch-thick cookies. Place on ungreased baking sheets; bake at 375 degrees for 13 minutes or until lightly golden. Mix meringue powder with water; brush on warm cookies. Mix crushed candy with remaining sugar; sprinkle candy mixture or coarse sugar over cookies. Makes 2 to 3 dozen.

Kathy McLaren
Visalia, CA

Lime Thumbprints

Refreshing lime adds just the right amount of flavor to these cookies!

½ c. butter, softened
¼ c. sugar
1 egg yolk

1½ t. vanilla extract
1¼ c. all-purpose flour
¼ t. salt

Beat butter, sugar, egg yolk and vanilla at medium speed with an electric mixer one to 2 minutes. Reduce speed to low; add flour and salt, blending well.

Shape dough into one-inch balls and place one inch apart on ungreased baking sheets. Make an indentation in the center of each ball using your thumb or the back of a teaspoon. Bake at 350 degrees for 12 to 15 minutes. Remove to a wire rack to cool completely. Spoon Lime Filling into centers of cookies. Makes about 2 dozen.

Lime Filling:

⅓ c. sugar
2 T. lime juice
1 T. lime zest

1 egg yolk
1 to 2 drops green food coloring

Combine first 4 ingredients in a small saucepan; heat over medium heat until mixture boils and begins to thicken, stirring constantly. Remove from heat; stir in food coloring. Set aside to cool to room temperature.

Cranberry-Pecan Coffee Cakes

These tender cranberry-and-nut streusel loaves are sure to please friends and neighbors.

½ c. butter, softened
1 c. sugar
2 eggs
2 c. all-purpose flour
2 t. baking powder
½ t. baking soda
½ t. salt

8-oz. container sour cream
1 t. almond extract
1 t. vanilla extract
16-oz. can whole-berry
  cranberry sauce
1 c. coarsely chopped pecans

Beat butter at medium speed with an electric mixer until creamy. Gradually add sugar, beating well. Add eggs, one at a time, beating until blended after each addition.

Combine flour and next 3 ingredients. Add flour mixture to butter mixture alternately with sour cream, beginning and ending with flour mixture. Stir in extracts.

Spoon ½ cup batter into each of 4 greased and floured 5"x3" mini loaf pans. Gently stir cranberry sauce; spoon 3 tablespoons over batter in each pan and spread lightly to edges; sprinkle 2 tablespoons pecans over cranberry sauce in each pan. Repeat layers in each pan using remaining batter, cranberry sauce and pecans.

Bake at 350 degrees for 48 to 50 minutes or until a toothpick inserted in center comes out clean. Cool in pans on a wire rack 15 minutes; remove from pans and let cool completely. Drizzle Almond Cream Glaze over cooled cakes. Makes 4 mini coffee cakes.

Almond Cream Glaze:

¾ c. powdered sugar
2 T. whipping cream

½ t. almond extract

Stir together all ingredients. Makes ⅓ cup.

Eggnog Cakes

½ c. pecans, finely chopped
18¼-oz. pkg. yellow cake mix
1 c. eggnog
¼ c. oil
3 eggs

2 T. orange juice
¼ t. nutmeg
2 c. powdered sugar
6 T. orange juice

Sprinkle 2 teaspoons chopped pecans into each of 9 generously greased and floured mini Bundt® pans; set aside.

Combine cake mix and next 5 ingredients in a large bowl; beat at medium speed with an electric mixer 2 minutes. Pour batter evenly into prepared pans.

Bake at 350 degrees for 25 minutes or until a toothpick inserted in center comes out clean. Cool in pans on wire racks 10 to 15 minutes; remove from pans and cool on wire racks.

Combine powdered sugar and orange juice in a small bowl; stir well. Drizzle glaze evenly over cakes. Makes 9 mini cakes.

quick cake tip

This recipe can also be made into one large cake. You'll need a 12-cup Bundt® pan. Follow the directions above, sprinkling all the pecans into a well-greased and floured pan. Proceed as directed; then bake at 350 degrees for 35 minutes or until a long wooden toothpick inserted in center of cake comes out clean. Serves 14.

Banana Pound Cake

This moist, full-flavored banana cake needs no ice cream or sauce to enhance its appeal. But if you insist, we recommend pralines-and-cream ice cream.

1½ c. butter, softened

3 c. sugar

5 eggs

3 ripe bananas, mashed

3 T. milk

2 t. vanilla extract

3 c. all-purpose flour

1 t. baking powder

½ t. salt

¾ c. chopped pecans

Beat butter at medium speed with an electric mixer about 2 minutes or until creamy. Gradually add sugar, beating 5 to 7 minutes. Add eggs, one at a time, beating just until yellow disappears after each addition.

Combine mashed bananas, milk and vanilla.

Combine flour, baking powder and salt; add to batter alternately with banana mixture, beginning and ending with flour mixture. Beat at low speed just until blended after each addition. Pour into a greased and floured 10" tube pan. Sprinkle with pecans.

Bake at 350 degrees for one hour and 20 minutes or until a long wooden pick inserted in center of cake comes out clean. Cool in pan on a wire rack 10 to 15 minutes; remove cake from pan and let cool completely on wire rack. Serves 10 to 12.

Mini Pumpkin Spice Loaves

¾ c. butter, softened
3 c. sugar
3 eggs
3 c. all-purpose flour
2 t. baking powder
1 t. baking soda
½ t. salt

1 t. cinnamon
1 t. ground cloves
¼ t. nutmeg
1 c. chopped pecans, toasted
¾ c. golden raisins
2 c. canned pumpkin
1 t. vanilla extract

Beat butter at medium speed with an electric mixer until creamy. Gradually add sugar, beating well. Add eggs, one at a time, beating just until yellow disappears after each addition.

Combine flour and next 6 ingredients in a medium bowl. Add pecans and raisins, tossing to coat. Add flour mixture to butter mixture alternately with pumpkin, beginning and ending with flour mixture. Stir in vanilla.

Spoon batter into 12 greased and floured 5"x3" mini loaf pans. Bake at 325 degrees for 45 minutes or until a toothpick inserted in center comes out clean. Cool in pans on a wire rack 10 minutes; remove from pans and let cool completely. Frost loaves with Cream Cheese Icing. Makes 12 mini loaves.

Cream Cheese Icing:

3-oz. pkg. cream cheese,
   softened
3 T. butter, softened

½ t. vanilla extract
2¾ c. powdered sugar
2 T. milk

Beat first 3 ingredients at medium speed with an electric mixer until creamy; gradually add powdered sugar, beating until smooth. Add milk, one tablespoon at a time, beating until spreading consistency. (Icing will be thick.) Makes 1¾ cup.

Christmas

Gingerbread

*Gingerbread
is a truly
old-fashioned
treat.*

Jo Ann

1 c. sugar
½ c. applesauce
¼ c. butter, softened or melted
¼ c. molasses
2 c. all-purpose flour
4 t. ground ginger

1 t. cinnamon
1 t. baking soda
¼ t. salt
1 c. fat-free buttermilk
2 eggs, lightly beaten
Optional: whipped cream

Beat first 4 ingredients at medium speed with an electric mixer until blended.

Stir together flour and next 4 ingredients in a medium bowl. Combine buttermilk and eggs in a separate bowl. Add both mixtures alternately to butter mixture, beginning and ending with flour mixture. Beat at low speed until blended after each addition. Pour batter into a lightly greased 10" cast-iron skillet.

Bake at 325 degrees for 35 to 40 minutes or until a toothpick inserted in center comes out clean. Garnish with whipped cream, if desired. Serves 8.

Jo Ann
Gooseberry Patch

Banana Bread

The best-tasting banana bread comes from using overripe bananas. Yogurt adds a nice tang to this recipe.

2 c. self-rising flour
1 c. sugar
¼ c. toasted wheat germ
½ t. baking soda
½ c. butter, melted

3 ripe bananas, mashed
2 eggs, lightly beaten
¼ c. strawberry yogurt or vanilla
   yogurt
1½ t. vanilla extract

Combine first 4 ingredients in a large bowl; make a well in center of mixture. Stir together melted butter, mashed banana, eggs, yogurt and vanilla. Add to dry ingredients; stir just until moistened. Pour batter into a greased and floured 9"x5" loaf pan.

Bake at 350 degrees for one hour and 5 minutes or until a toothpick inserted in center comes out clean. Cover loosely with aluminum foil after 40 minutes if loaf begins to brown too quickly. Cool in pan on a wire rack 10 minutes; remove from pan and cool completely on wire rack. Makes one loaf.

Note: For muffins, spoon batter into lightly greased or paper-lined muffin cups, filling ¾ full. Bake at 350 degrees for 19 to 21 minutes or until golden. Remove from pans immediately. Let cool on wire racks. Makes 20 muffins.

Chocolate Granola Brittle

The beauty of this recipe is that you can make a decadent brittle in the microwave in half the time it takes to make the traditional candy. If you want to make more than one pound, don't double the recipe...it won't give you the same result. Just make it twice.

1 c. sugar
½ c. light corn syrup
⅛ t. salt
1 c. pecans, coarsely chopped
1 T. butter
1 t. vanilla extract

1 t. baking soda
¾ c. chocolate granola
3 (1-oz.) sqs. semi-sweet baking
   chocolate
1½ T. shortening

Combine first 3 ingredients in a 2-quart glass bowl. Microwave on high 5 minutes. Stir in pecans. Microwave 1½ minutes. Stir in butter and vanilla. Microwave one minute and 45 seconds or until candy is the color of peanut butter. Stir in baking soda (mixture will bubble).

Quickly pour candy onto a lightly greased rimless baking sheet. (Pour as thinly as possible without spreading candy.) Cover brittle quickly with parchment paper and use a rolling pin to thin out candy; peel off parchment. Sprinkle granola over brittle. Replace parchment and use rolling pin to press granola into brittle; peel off parchment. Cool brittle completely; break into pieces.

Place chocolate squares and shortening in a small bowl. Microwave on high, 1½ to 2 minutes, stirring after one minute. Dip each piece of brittle halfway into chocolate mixture. Place dipped brittle on parchment paper to harden. Store in an airtight container. Makes about one pound.

English Toffee

1 c. butter
1⅓ c. sugar
1 T. light corn syrup
3 T. water

2½ c. slivered almonds, finely chopped, toasted and divided
3 (1.55-oz.) milk chocolate candy bars, divided

Line a 13"x9" baking pan with aluminum foil. Butter foil; set aside.

Combine first 4 ingredients in a 4-quart heavy saucepan. Cook over medium-low heat until mixture comes to a boil. Wash down crystals from sides of pan with a small brush dipped in hot water. Cook mixture until it reaches the hard-crack stage, or 290 to 310 degrees on a candy thermometer, stirring occasionally to prevent scorching. Remove from heat and stir in 1½ cups almonds. Spread mixture in prepared pan; cool completely (about 30 minutes).

Break 1½ chocolate bars into pieces and place in a small glass bowl. Microwave on high 50 seconds; stir until chocolate melts. Spread melted chocolate over toffee mixture; sprinkle with ½ cup almonds. Let cool until set (about one hour). Lift foil and candy from pan. Place a 15"x10" jelly-roll pan over candy and invert candy onto jelly-roll pan; remove foil.

Melt remaining chocolate bars as above. Spread melted chocolate over toffee; sprinkle with remaining almonds. Chill, uncovered, 30 minutes or until firm; break into pieces. Makes about 2 pounds.

Rochelle Sundholm
Creswell, OR

Chocolate-Covered Espresso Beans

1 c. espresso beans
12-oz. pkg. dark chocolate chips,
  melted

12-oz. pkg. semi-sweet
  chocolate chips, melted

Place espresso beans about ½ inch apart in a wax paper-lined jelly-roll pan; spoon melted dark chocolate over beans. Chill in refrigerator until hard; turn beans over and spoon melted semi-sweet chocolate over beans. Repeat chilling. Makes one cup.

Vickie
Gooseberry Patch

A great gift for your coffee-loving friends!

Vickie

made by hand

Fill a mini box with all the essentials for making handmade cards...scraps of vintage floral fabrics, buttons, colorful card stock, ribbon, a glue stick, envelopes and stamps. Tie up this pretty package with a ribbon threaded through a decorative buckle or brooch.

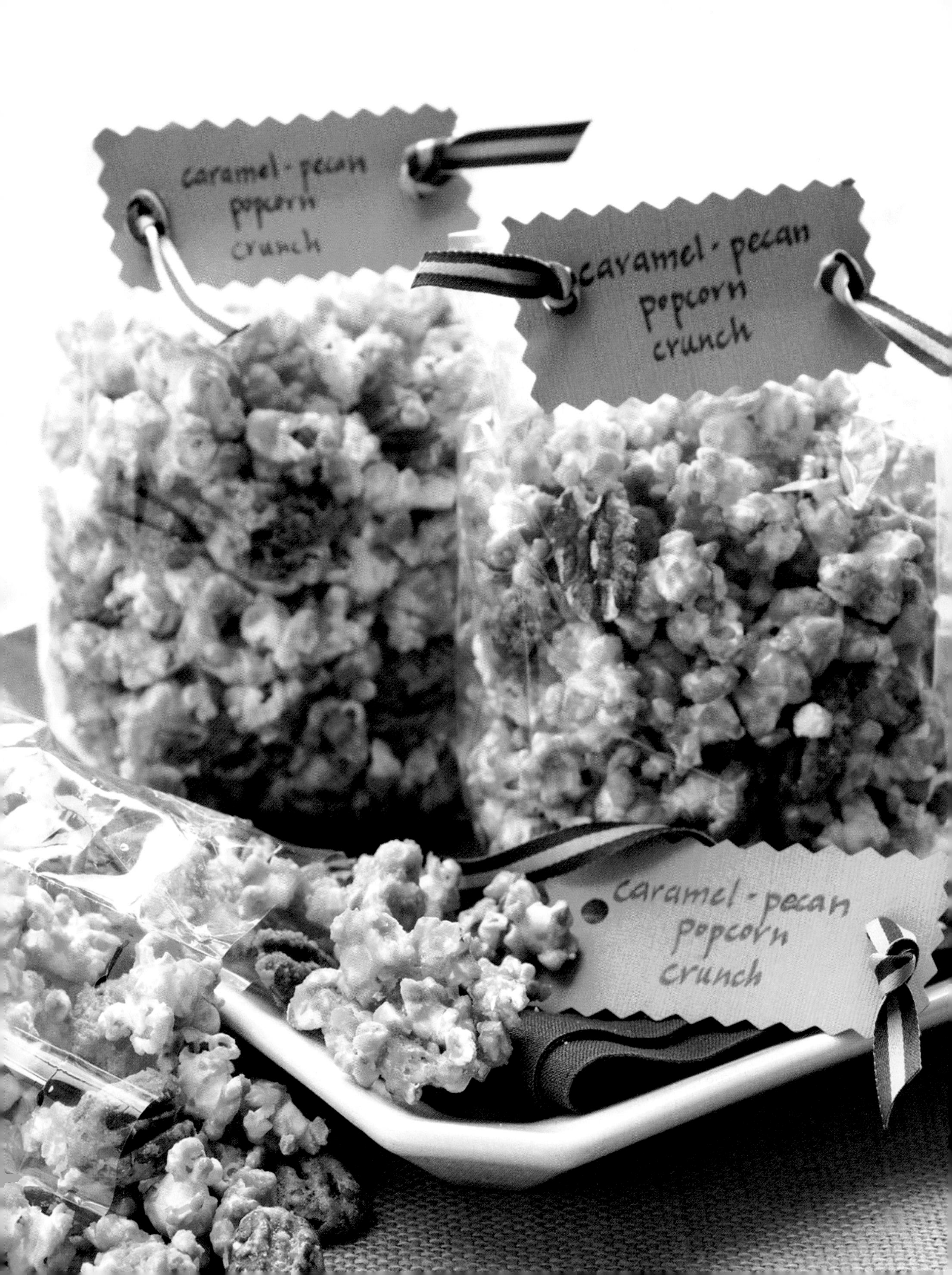

Caramel-Pecan Popcorn Crunch

These crisp, buttery popcorn clusters with toasted pecans rival any sweet popcorn snack you can buy at the store.

2 c. pecan halves
2 (3½-oz.) pkgs. natural-flavored microwave popcorn, popped
2 c. light brown sugar, packed
½ c. butter

½ c. light corn syrup
2 t. vanilla extract
½ t. almond extract
½ t. salt
½ t. baking soda

Bake pecans in a single layer in a shallow pan at 350 degrees for 8 to 10 minutes or until lightly toasted and fragrant.

Reduce oven temperature to 250 degrees. Combine popcorn and pecans in a lightly greased 16"x12"x3" roasting pan.

Combine brown sugar, butter and corn syrup in a 2½-quart heavy saucepan. Bring to a boil over medium-high heat, stirring until butter melts. Wash down sides of pan with a brush dipped in hot water. Cook mixture until it reaches the hard-ball stage, or 250 to 269 degrees on a candy thermometer, about 4 minutes. (Do not stir.)

Remove from heat; stir in extracts, salt and baking soda. Gradually pour brown sugar mixture over popcorn and nuts, stirring gently to coat well, using a long-handled spoon.

Bake at 250 degrees for 1½ hours or until dry, stirring occasionally. Cool completely in pan. Break into clusters and store in an airtight container up to 2 weeks. Makes 25 cups.

money-saving tip

It's often more economical to buy packaged popcorn kernels than microwave popcorn. Use ⅔ cup unpopped popcorn kernels for this recipe. Pop kernels according to package directions.

Thanksgiving

Cookie Dough Truffles

This chocolate chip cookie dough comes in candy form, wrapped in a chocolate shell.

½ c. butter, softened
½ c. brown sugar, packed
¼ c. sugar
¼ c. egg substitute
1 t. vanilla extract
1¼ c. all-purpose flour

1 c. mini semi-sweet chocolate chips
¾ c. chopped pecans or walnuts
12-oz. pkg. semi-sweet chocolate chips
1½ T. shortening

Beat butter at medium speed with an electric mixer until creamy; gradually add sugars, beating well. Add egg substitute and vanilla; beat well. Add flour to butter mixture; beat well. Stir in mini chocolate chips and chopped pecans. Cover and chill 30 minutes.

Shape mixture into one-inch balls. Cover and freeze balls until very firm.

Place chocolate chips and shortening in a one-quart glass bowl; melt in microwave according to package directions. Using 2 forks, quickly dip frozen truffles into melted chocolate, coating completely. Place on wax paper to harden. Store truffles in refrigerator up to 3 days. Makes 4½ dozen.

Merry Cherry Fudge

36 maraschino cherries with
   stems, juice reserved
12-oz. pkg. semi-sweet
   chocolate chips
6 (1-oz.) sqs. bittersweet baking
   chocolate, chopped

14-oz. can sweetened
   condensed milk
1 c. chopped pecans

This easy fudge recipe has a sweet cherry in every square...scrumptious!

Jo Ann

Lightly coat an 8"x8" pan with non-stick vegetable spray; set aside. Blot cherries dry with paper towels.

Combine chocolates in a heavy saucepan; place over very low heat and stir until melted and smooth. Remove from heat and stir in sweetened condensed milk and one teaspoon reserved cherry juice. Stir in pecans. Spoon mixture into prepared pan. Immediately press cherries into fudge, leaving top of each cherry and stem exposed. Cover and chill fudge 2 hours. Cut fudge into 36 squares. Store in an airtight container in refrigerator. Makes 2 pounds.

Jo Ann
Gooseberry Patch

chocolate cutouts

Mini cookie cutters are just the right size to make chocolate cutouts. Pour melted semi-sweet chocolate onto wax paper-lined baking sheets and spread to ⅛-inch thickness. Refrigerate until firm and then cut shapes with cookie cutters. Remove from wax paper and chill...a sweet garnish on a frosted cake!

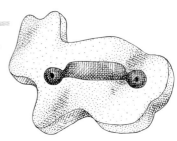

White Chocolate Cookies 'n' Cream Fudge

1 c. sugar
¾ c. butter
5-oz. can evaporated milk
2 (12-oz.) pkgs. white chocolate
   chips

7-oz. jar marshmallow creme
25 chocolate sandwich cookies,
   coarsely crushed and divided
⅛ t. salt

Line a greased 9"x9" baking pan with aluminum foil; set aside.

Combine first 3 ingredients in a medium saucepan. Cook over medium-high heat, stirring constantly, until mixture comes to a boil; cook 3 minutes, stirring constantly. Remove from heat; add white chocolate chips, marshmallow creme, 2 cups crushed cookies and salt. Stir until chips melt.

Pour fudge into prepared pan. Sprinkle remaining one cup cookies over fudge, gently pressing cookies into fudge. Cover and chill until firm (about one to 2 hours).

Lift uncut fudge in aluminum foil from pan; remove foil and cut fudge into squares. Makes 4 pounds.

Peppermint-White Chocolate Candy Bars

24 red and green hard
    peppermint round candies
2 (12-oz.) pkgs. white chocolate
    chips

1 t. peppermint extract

Line 3 (9"x5") loaf pans with plastic wrap; set aside. Place candies in a plastic zipping bag. Coarsely crush candies using a rolling pin. Set aside crushed candies, reserving 3 tablespoons for topping.

Microwave white chocolate chips in a large microwave-safe bowl on medium (70%) one minute and 15 seconds. (Chips will not look melted.) Stir chips until melted. Microwave again in 15-second intervals, if necessary. Add peppermint extract and larger portion of crushed candies to melted chocolate, stirring until evenly distributed.

Quickly spread melted white chocolate evenly in prepared pans; sprinkle with reserved 3 tablespoons candies, pressing gently with fingertips. Let stand one hour or until firm. Makes 3 bars.

Peanut Brittle Candy Bars:

Melt white chocolate as directed in recipe above, gently folding in 1½ cups crushed store-bought peanut brittle and ½ cup creamy peanut butter; spread evenly in prepared loaf pans. Dollop one tablespoon creamy peanut butter over candy mixture in each loaf pan; swirl with a knife. Sprinkle ½ cup crushed peanut brittle evenly over candy in pans, pressing gently with fingertips. Makes 3 bars.

Hello Dolly Candy Bars:

Measure and combine ⅔ cup each mini semisweet chocolate chips, toasted flaked coconut, chopped pecans, and chopped graham crackers; set aside ½ cup of this mix for topping. Melt white chocolate as directed in recipe above, gently folding in combined ingredients; spread evenly in prepared loaf pans. Sprinkle reserved ½ cup topping mixture over candy in pans, pressing gently with fingertips. Makes 3 bars.

Herbed Shrimp Tacos, page 48

celebration menus

Need ideas for the perfect dishes to serve at your next holiday gathering? Look no further! In this chapter you'll find 16 complete menus to prepare for your favorite celebrations throughout the year. We've even included a photo with each menu to inspire perfect results! From a casual New Year's Day lunch with family & friends (page 314) to an Easter Sunday brunch fit for a crowd (page 311), your holiday meal planning is all set!

New Year's Eve Dinner Party

serves 12

Seafood Gumbo (page 123)

French bread

Bread Pudding (page 249)

Champagne

Christmas Brunch for a Crowd

serves 16

*Cheese & Chile Casserole
(page 76)*

chicken-apple sausage links

*Orange Coffee Rolls (page 203)

coffee, tea & hot chocolate

*Double recipe.

Thanksgiving Day Buffet

serves 12

Deep-Fried Turkey (page 57)

*Holiday Yams (page 169)

*Apple-Broccoli Salad (page 183)

dinner rolls

*Perfect Pecan Pie (page 241)

*Double recipe.

Haunted House Dessert Party

serves 16

Caramel Apple Crisp (page 247)

*Marshmallow Cookie Spiders
(page 250)

Pumpkin Spice Bars (page 257)

Caramel-Pecan Popcorn Crunch
(page 299)

*Double recipe.

Labor Day Picnic Lunch

serves 8

Mother's Fried Chicken (page 87)

corn on the cob

potato salad

Watermelon Fruitsicles (page 263)

assorted beverages

Fathers' Day BBQ

serves 6 to 8

Easy Southern-Style Pork Barbecue (page 144)

coleslaw

potato chips

Peanut Butter-Ice Cream Pie (page 246)

Fiesta Night

serves 10

Herbed Shrimp Tacos (page 48)

guacamole

margaritas

*Lemon-Coconut Bars
(page 258)*

Easter Sunday
Brunch

serves 18

**Garden-Fresh Egg Casserole
(page 43)*

Whole Baked Ham (page 59)

breakfast rolls

Pretty Little Cakes (page 230)

*Double recipe.

Christmas Eve
Cookie Swap

serves about 20

*Chocolate-Caramel Thumbprints
(page 255)*

Big Crunchy Sugar Cookies (page 279)

Mom's Gingerbread Cookies (page 281)

Brownie Buttons (page 283)

hot chocolate

Trick-or-Treat
Supper

serves 8

*Eyeball Soup in a Slow Cooker
(page 132)*

mixed greens salad

Jack-o'-Lantern Bread (page 199)

orange soda

4th of July Dinner

serves 4

Firecracker Grilled Salmon
(page 49)

cucumber & tomato salad

lemonade

Speedy Sorbet (page 262)

Down-Home Dinner for Dad

serves 4

Ultimate Cheeseburger Pizza
(page 71)

Tempting Caesar Salad (page 176)

soda

Chocolate-Caramel Sheet Cake
(page 226)

Turkey Day Dinner

serves 12

Roast Turkey & Gravy (page 92)

Cornbread Dressing (page 156)

*Roasted Sweet Potato Salad (page 183)

buttered green beans

Pumpkin Pie Ice Cream Fantasy
(page 265)

*Double recipe.

New Year's Day
Southern Lunch

serves 4 to 6

Hearty Black-Eyed Peas (page 61)

cooked rice

cornbread

iced tea

Warm Turtle Cake (page 218)

Mothers' Day Brunch

serves 8

*Turkey-Veggie Bagels
(page 137)

fruit salad

Mile-High Frozen Strawberry Pie
(page 246)

*Double recipe.

Easter Egg Hunt Picnic

serves 6 to 8

Mark's Egg Salad Sandwiches
(page 135)

pasta salad

Mom Ford's Chocolate Chip Cookies
(page 250)

assorted beverages

METRIC EQUIVALENTS

The recipes that appear in this cookbook use the standard U.S. method for measuring liquid and dry or solid ingredients (teaspoons, tablespoons, and cups). The information in the following charts is provided to help cooks outside the United States successfully use these recipes. All equivalents are approximate.

METRIC EQUIVALENTS FOR DIFFERENT TYPES OF INGREDIENTS

A standard cup measure of a dry or solid ingredient will vary in weight depending on the type of ingredient.
A standard cup of liquid is the same volume for any type of liquid. Use the following chart when converting standard cup measures to grams (weight) or milliliters (volume).

Standard Cup	Fine Powder (ex. flour)	Grain (ex. rice)	Granular (ex. sugar)	Liquid Solids (ex. butter)	Liquid (ex. milk)
1	140 g	150 g	190 g	200 g	240 ml
¾	105 g	113 g	143 g	150 g	180 ml
⅔	93 g	100 g	125 g	133 g	160 ml
½	70 g	75 g	95 g	100 g	120 ml
⅓	47 g	50 g	63 g	67 g	80 ml
¼	35 g	38 g	48 g	50 g	60 ml
⅛	18 g	19 g	24 g	25 g	30 ml

USEFUL EQUIVALENTS FOR LIQUID INGREDIENTS BY VOLUME

¼ tsp	=						1 ml
½ tsp	=						2 ml
1 tsp	=						5 ml
3 tsp	=	1 tbls			= ½ fl oz	=	15 ml
		2 tbls	=	⅛ cup	= 1 fl oz	=	30 ml
		4 tbls	=	¼ cup	= 2 fl oz	=	60 ml
		5⅓ tbls	=	⅓ cup	= 3 fl oz	=	80 ml
		8 tbls	=	½ cup	= 4 fl oz	=	120 ml
		10⅔ tbls	=	⅔ cup	= 5 fl oz	=	160 ml
		12 tbls	=	¾ cup	= 6 fl oz	=	180 ml
		16 tbls	=	1 cup	= 8 fl oz	=	240 ml
		1 pt	=	2 cups	= 16 fl oz	=	480 ml
		1 qt	=	4 cups	= 32 fl oz	=	960 ml
					33 fl oz	=	1000 ml = 1 liter

USEFUL EQUIVALENTS FOR DRY INGREDIENTS BY WEIGHT

(To convert ounces to grams, multiply the number of ounces by 30.)

1 oz	=	⅟₁₆ lb	=	30 g
4 oz	=	¼ lb	=	120 g
8 oz	=	½ lb	=	240 g
12 oz	=	¾ lb	=	360 g
16 oz	=	1 lb	=	480 g

USEFUL EQUIVALENTS FOR LENGTH

(To convert inches to centimeters, multiply the number of inches by 2.5.)

1 in =		= 2.5 cm	
6 in = ½ ft		= 15 cm	
12 in = 1 ft		= 30 cm	
36 in = 3 ft = 1 yd		= 90 cm	
40 in =		= 100 cm	= 1 meter

USEFUL EQUIVALENTS FOR COOKING/OVEN TEMPERATURES

	Fahrenheit	Celsius	Gas Mark
Freeze Water	32° F	0° C	
Room Temperature	68° F	20° C	
Boil Water	212° F	100° C	
Bake	325° F	160° C	3
	350° F	180° C	4
	375° F	190° C	5
	400° F	200° C	6
	425° F	220° C	7
	450° F	230° C	8
Broil			Grill

index

appetizers & snacks

Aloha Chicken Wings, 18
Baked Spinach & Artichoke Dip, 26
Black Bean Tartlets, 34
Black-Eyed Caviar, 31
Brie Kisses, 22
Caramel Apples, 37
Caramelized Vidalia Onion Dip, 17
Chunky Guacamole, 31
Citrus Mimosa, 15
Curly Pigtails, 19
Curried Chicken Salad Tea Sandwiches, 33
Egg Salad Crostini, 30
Fresh Salsa, 33
Ham-Cream Cheese Croissants, 22
Homemade Eggnog, 14
Iced Mint Tea, 15
Not-Your-Usual Party Mix, 35
Peppermint Milkshakes, 13
Pineapple Ball, 29
Pineapple Wassail, 10
Puppy Chow Snack Mix...For People!, 35
Roasted Red Pepper Bruschetta, 23
Snow Cocoa, 10
Spicy Crawfish Spread, 25
Stuffed Strawberries, 29
Sweet Almond Coffee, 11
Ultimate Nachos, 21
Yuletide Crab Puffs, 27

breads

Almond French Toast, 212
Autumn Apple Cakes, 213
Banana Bread, 293
Banana Bread French Toast, 41

Barley Quick Bread, 188
Best-Ever Soft Pretzels, 200
Blueberry 'n' Cheese Coffee Cake, 215
Broccoli Cornbread, 196
Buttermilk 'n' Honey Pancakes, 40
Chocolate Bread, 201
Cream Cheese Braids, 209
Croutons, 176
Dakota Bread, 189
Gingerbread, 292
Ginger Scones, 211
Harvest Pumpkin Bread, 208
Herbed Fan Dinner Rolls, 193
Jack-o'-Lantern Bread, 199
Lemony Poppy Seed Bread, 208
Matzo Balls, 124
Melt-in-Your-Mouth Rolls, 192
Mini Pumpkin Spice Loaves, 291
Orange Coffee Rolls, 203
Parsley Biscuits, 196
Pimento Cheese Biscuits, 195
Savory Sausage-Swiss Muffins, 197
Sticky Bun Biscuits, 205
Streusel Cran-Orange Muffins, 207
Sugar-Topped Muffins, 207
Sweet Potato Biscuits, 204
Whole-Wheat Popovers, 191

cakes

Apple Spice Cake, 223
Aunt Neal's Old-Fashioned Tea Cakes, 280
Banana Pound Cake, 289
Caramel Cake, 221
Chocolate-Cappuccino Cheesecake, 238
Chocolate-Caramel Sheet Cake, 226
Cookies 'n' Cream Cake, 235
Cranberry-Ginger Crumble Cake, 234
Cranberry-Pecan Coffee Cakes, 287
Eggnog Cakes, 288
Jumbo Chocolate Cupcakes, 229
Million-Dollar Pound Cake, 233
Mini Cheesecakes, 239
Mom's Special Occasion Cherry Cake, 219
Patriotic Cupcakes, 227
Peppermint Candy Cheesecake, 237
Pretty Little Cakes, 230
Pumpkin Cake Roll, 231
Red Velvet Layer Cake, 222
Warm Turtle Cake, 218
White Christmas Coconut Sheet
    Cake, 225

candies & confections

Caramel-Pecan Popcorn Crunch, 299
Chocolate-Covered Espresso Beans, 297
Chocolate Granola Brittle, 295
Cookie Dough Truffles, 300
Dipped & Drizzled Pretzels, 277
English Toffee, 296
Hello Dolly Candy Bars, 305
Merry Cherry Fudge, 301
Peanut Brittle Candy Bars, 305
Peppermint-White Chocolate Candy
    Bars, 305
Spicy Vanilla Pecans, 276
Toffee Peanuts, 275
White Chocolate Cookies 'n' Cream
    Fudge, 303

cookies & bars

Big Crunchy Sugar Cookies, 279
Brownie Buttons, 283
Buckeye Brownies, 261
Chocolate-Caramel Thumbprints, 255
Jo Ann's Walnut-Oatmeal Cookie
    Mix, 277
Lemon-Coconut Bars, 258
Lime Thumbprints, 285
Macaroon Tartlets, 254
Marshmallow Cookie Spiders, 250
Mom Ford's Chocolate Chip Cookies, 250
Mom's Gingerbread Cookies, 281
Peppermint Pinwheels, 284
Pumpkin Spice Bars, 257
Raspberry Bars, 259
Sugar Cookies, 253
Vanilla-Dipped Gingersnaps, 251
Yummy Cappuccino Bites, 254

desserts

Bread Pudding, 249
Caramel Apple Crisp, 247
Pucker Pops, 262
Pumpkin Pie Ice Cream Fantasy, 265
Speedy Sorbet, 262
Vickie's Chocolate Fondue, 261
Watermelon Fruitsicles, 263

entrées

Almond-and-Herb-Crusted Trout, 80
Apricot-Glazed Pork Tenderloin &
    Couscous, 96
Bacon-Wrapped Burgers, 69
Baked Sausage & Eggs, 105
Cheese & Chile Casserole, 76
Chicken-Fried Steak, 113
Chicken Lasagna with Roasted Red Pepper
    Sauce, 52
Chicken Pot Pie, 88
Christmas Breakfast Stratas, 64
Christmas Morning Chile Relleno, 43
Chunky Ham Pot Pie, 60
Corn Dogs, 67
Cox's Memphis-in-May Ribs, 95
Cranberry Meatloaves, 104
Cranberry-Orange Glazed Cornish
    Hens, 93
Creamy Beef Stroganoff, 72
Creamy Chicken à la King, 84
Deep-Fried Turkey, 57
Divine Chicken & Wild Rice
    Casserole, 51
Fabulous Fajitas, 53
Festive Cajun Pepper Steak, 11
Festive Pork Roasts, 101
Filet Mignon with Mushrooms, 109
Firecracker Grilled Salmon, 49
Fruited Pork Loin, 97
Garden-Fresh Egg Casserole, 43
Garlicky Baked Shrimp, 47

Grilled Chicken with White BBQ Sauce, 55
Ham with Bourbon, Cola & Cherry
    Glaze, 103
Hearty Black-Eyed Peas, 61
Herbed Shrimp Tacos, 48
Hickory-Smoked Kabobs, 73
Honey-Glazed Turkey Breast, 56
Juicy Prime Rib, 109
Laurie's Stuffed Peppers, 79
Linguine & White Clam Sauce, 45
Maple Roast Chicken & Veggies, 85
Mexican Lasagna, 107
Mother's Fried Chicken, 87
Mustard-Crusted Pork Roast & Browned
    Potatoes, 100
Party Paella Casserole, 83
Pork Chops, Cabbage & Apples, 99
Pork Chops & Rice Skillet, 65
Red Beans & Rice, 63
Rich Seafood Casserole, 81
Roast Turkey & Gravy, 92
Shiitake Mushroom & Spinach
    Manicotti, 77
Spicy Pasta Alfredo Casserole, 44
Spinach-Cheddar Quiche, 104
Sweet-and-Spicy Glazed Turkey, 91
Tenderloin for Two with Peppercorn
    Cream, 108
Tried & True Meatloaf, 68
Turkey & Wild Rice Casserole, 89
Ultimate Cheeseburger Pizza, 71
Whole Baked Ham, 59

frostings, fillings & toppings

5-Cup Cream Cheese Frosting, 222
Almond Cream Glaze, 287
Butter Frosting, 219
Caramel Glaze, 223
Cream Cheese Icing, 291
Filling, 231
Frosting, 235
Lemon Chess Pie Filling, 258
Lime Filling, 285
Nutmeg Sauce, 231
Powdered Sugar Frosting, 281
Quick Caramel Frosting, 226
Rum Sauce, 249
Sugar Cookie Frosting, 253
Thick Chocolate Frosting, 229
Whipped Cream Caramel Frosting, 221

pies & pastries

Apple Pie in a Jar, 273
Bar Harbor Cranberry Pie, 243
Chocolate Marshmallow Pie, 242
Mile-High Frozen Strawberry Pie, 246
Mocha Pecan Mud Pie, 245
New England Pumpkin Pie, 242
Peanut Butter-Ice Cream Pie, 246
Perfect Pecan Pie, 241

salads & dressings

Apple-Broccoli Salad, 183
Cashew Salad, 177
Cranberry Relish Salad, 173
Fresh Corn Salad, 185
Layered Cornbread & Turkey
    Salad, 180
Lettuce Wedge Salad, 175
Roasted Sweet Potato Salad, 183
Spinach-Pecan Salad, 179
Sweet Pineapple Coleslaw, 181
Tempting Caesar Salad, 176

sandwiches

Creamy Tuna Melts, 136
Cucumber Sandwiches, 133
Delicious BBQ Hamburgers, 144
Easy Southern-Style Pork
    Barbecue, 144
Fancy Chicken Salad, 136
Grilled Cuban Sandwiches, 143
Mark's Egg Salad Sandwiches, 135
Scrumptious Sandwich
    Loaves, 141
Slow Cooker Sloppy Joes, 145
Tailgate Party Sandwiches, 140
Toasty Ham & Swiss Stacks, 140
Turkey Panini, 139
Turkey-Veggie Bagels, 137

sauces & condiments

Barbecue Sauce, 95
Festive Cranberry Honey, 271
Go-Team Chili Seasoning, 268
Homemade Maple Syrup, 271
Olive Pesto, 269
Sun-Dried Tomato & Roasted Garlic
    Pesto, 269
Ultimate Fudge Sauce, 272

side dishes

3-Cheese Pasta Bake, 171
Au Gratin Potato Casserole, 164
Baked Butternut Squash & Apples, 153
Black-Eyed Peas with Caramelized
    Onions & Country Ham, 160
Brussels Sprouts au Gratin, 152
Butter Beans with Cornbread
    Crust, 149
Corn Pudding, 155
Cornbread Dressing, 156
Creamy Southern Grits, 168
Crumb-Topped Spinach
    Casserole, 165
Dad's Braggin' Beans, 148
Easy Fancy Broccoli, 151
Fruited Curry Rice Bake, 172
Garlic-Basil Mashed Potatoes, 161
Glazed Carrots, 153
Green Bean-Corn Casserole, 157
Holiday Yams, 169
Homestyle Green Beans, 159
Perfect Potato Latkes, 164
Roasted Vegetables, 168
Scalloped Potatoes with Ham, 163
Squash Casserole, 167

soups & stews

30-Minute Chili, 131
Butternut Squash Soup, 120
Black Beans 'n' Vegetable Chili, 116
Chicken & Wild Rice Soup, 125
Chicken Tortilla Soup, 127
Chili Seasoning Mix, 131
Chow-Down Corn Chowder, 129
Christmas Luncheon Crabmeat
    Bisque, 121
Easy Brunswick Stew, 129
Easy Slow Cooker Potato Soup, 117
Eyeball Soup in a Slow Cooker, 132
Matzo Ball Soup, 124
Seafood Gumbo, 123
Tomato-Basil Soup, 117
Turkey-Vegetable Chowder, 128
Whole Acorn Squash Cream Soup, 119

Our Story

ack in 1984, we were next-door neighbors raising our families in the little town of Delaware, Ohio. We were two moms with small children looking for a way to do what we loved and stay home with the kids too. We shared a love of home cooking and making memories with family & friends. After many a conversation over the backyard fence, **Gooseberry Patch** was born.

We put together the first catalog & cookbooks at our kitchen tables and packed boxes from the basement, enlisting the help of our loved ones wherever we could. From that little family, we've grown to include an amazing group of creative folks who love cooking, decorating and creating as much as we do.

Hard to believe it's been over 25 years since those kitchen-table days. Today, we're best known for our homestyle, family-friendly cookbooks. We love hand-picking the recipes and are tickled to share our inspiration, ideas and more with you! One thing's for sure, we couldn't have done it without our friends all across the country. Whether you've been along for the ride from the beginning or are just discovering us, welcome to our family!

Your friends at Gooseberry Patch

Find us here too!

Join our **Circle of Friends** and discover free recipes & crafts, plus giveaways & more! Visit our website or blog to join and be sure to follow us on Facebook & Twitter too.

www.gooseberrypatch.com